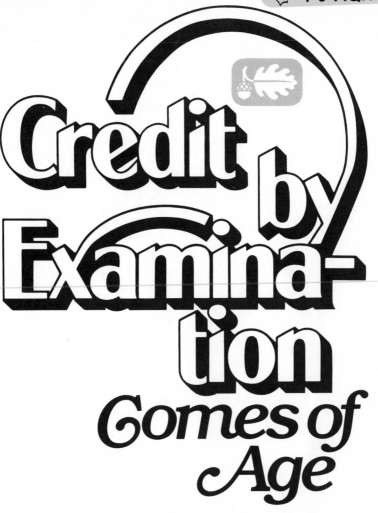

Credit by Examination Comes of Age

Implications of AP and CLEP for Colleges, Schools, and Students

*Report of the Colloquium on Credit by Examination
at the University of Wisconsin – Madison,
on March 7–9, 1979*

College Entrance Examination Board, New York, 1980

Copies of this book may be ordered from College Board
Publication Orders, Box 2815, Princeton, New Jersey 08541.
The price is $10.95.

Editorial inquiries concerning this book should be directed
to Editorial Office, The College Board, 888 Seventh Avenue,
New York, New York 10019.

Book design by Lucy M. Fehr
Cover design by Terrence M. Fehr
Photographs by Gary Schultz of the University of Wisconsin

Contents

Introduction

This book is based on a national invitational colloquium that took place March 7–9, 1979, at the University of Wisconsin – Madison. Sponsored by the College Board in cooperation with the Committee on Institutional Cooperation of the Big Ten Universities and the University of Chicago (CIC), the colloquium afforded a timely opportunity to consider the ends achieved and the difficulties created by the use of examinations of the Advanced Placement Program (APP) and the College-Level Examination Program (CLEP) as avenues to college credit. The book includes the papers that were commissioned on various aspects of credit by examination to stimulate and inform discussion at the colloquium; other sections of the book convey a sense of the substance and also the flavor of the discussion itself. The names of those who engaged in the discussion and gave life to the colloquium are also included.

The idea for such a colloquium grew out of a series of conversations within the staff of the Board and its Council on College-Level Services regarding special efforts the Board might undertake to bring about among school and college administrators and faculty members both a deeper interest in, and a wider consensus of views with respect to, various aspects and implications of credit by examination. Although AP and CLEP examinations were increasingly being used by many colleges, some institutions had little or no experience with them, and they were a source of frustration or confusion for some colleges, schools, and students.

The particular appeal of a colloquium was its responsiveness to two of the purposes of the College Board as stated in its charter: one, to provide a forum for the discussion by colleges and schools of their common problems, and the other, to develop representative opinion with respect to educational standards.

Once it was decided to sponsor a colloquium, the cooperation of the Committee on Institutional Cooperation was enlisted in the search for an appropriate site. The CIC has a long and active record of efforts in support of credit by examination. Through Fred H. Jackson, director of CIC, arrangements were made with Wilson Thiede, provost, University Outreach, University of Wisconsin, to use the University Bay Center at Madison as the site for the colloquium.

Prospects for the colloquium brightened further when Lorrin Kennamer, dean of the College of Education, University of Texas at Austin, agreed to serve as colloquium leader. Mr. Kennamer had been a member of the original Council on College-Level Examinations of the College Board and more recently had served as chairman of the College Board. Both he and Mr. Jackson joined a small group of advisers who met at the Board offices in May 1978 to lay out plans for the colloquium. Other members of the planning group were Raymond Brokamp, assistant superintendent, Cincinnati Public Schools; Ernest Ern, vice president of student affairs, University of Virginia; Caryl Kline, secretary of education, Pennsylvania State Department of Education; Donald Kreider, professor of mathematics, Dartmouth College; Frank McKean, dean of student affairs and services, University of Utah; and Douglas Whitney, American Council on Education, Washington, D.C.

A major task of the planning group was to identify topics on which papers would be commissioned for discussion at the colloquium. The contents of this book reflect their decisions in this regard. The group also considered the kinds of individuals needed at the colloquium to provide the right mix of institutional, professional, and personal viewpoints. They agreed that secondary schools should be represented as well as postsecondary institutions and that faculty members and others with academic responsibilities should be there along with admissions officers, counselors, registrars, and testing officers, whose work is directly affected by credit by examination. They hoped that participants would include students, critics and also advocates of credit by examination, and persons with limited AP and CLEP experience as well as others whose experience was extensive.

A three-stage approach was adopted in hopes of bringing about such a mix of participants. As a first step, Robert F. Kingston, president of the College Board, wrote to the chief officers of the more than 2,400 member colleges and schools in November 1978, informing them of plans for the colloquium and inviting them to send him the names of individuals to whom registration materials would be sent later. More than 300 names were received in response. The second step was to mail registration forms to the individuals so named along with information about the colloquium. The third and most suspenseful stage was waiting to see how many in fact would register and who they would turn out to be. The 140 registrations eventually received from all regions of the country exceeded expectations as to number, and as gratifying as the number of registrants was their diversity. Included were principals, headmasters, teachers, counselors, and directors of instruction at many secondary schools; and academic officers, faculty members, admissions officers, registrars, and testing officers at both public and private colleges and universities.

Swelling this basic group of colloquium participants were officials, faculty members, and students at the University of Wisconsin to whom special invitations were extended; several special guests; present or former members of College Board committees; and College Board and Educational Testing Service staff members.

Once assembled on March 7, with Mr. Kennamer presiding, participants were welcomed by Mr. Thiede on behalf of the University of Wisconsin, Mr. Jackson on behalf of the CIC, and Albert G. Sims on behalf of the College Board. Activities from then on alternated between plenary sessions, at which papers were summarized by their authors and discussed, and meetings of small discussion groups, to which participants were assigned. Representatives of these small groups reported the outcomes of their discussions at a plenary session near the end of the colloquium. During the final session Jack N. Arbolino presented his remarks in tribute to the "dreamers" who helped to make credit by examination a reality in this country, and Mr. Kennamer summarized the ideas and concerns he had heard participants express and his own perspective with respect to the future of credit by examination.

The list of those who had a hand in shaping and bringing

about this colloquium is very long. The colloquium provided those who participated in it a remarkable opportunity to expand their understanding of credit by examination at a critical stage in its evolution. This book captures so much of the colloquium that readers now have a comparable opportunity, and for this, major credit goes to Diane L. Olsen, the editor.

John A. Valentine
Professional Associate
for Academic Affairs
The College Board

1

Why does credit by examination demand serious attention?

What are the origins of APP and CLEP? How are they similar, and how are they different?

Donald L. Kreider, currently a professor of mathematics at Dartmouth College and a past vice president of the college, received a Ph.D. in mathematics from the Massachusetts Institute of Technology. He is a member of several College Board committees on mathematics, and his many professional affiliations include offices in the Mathematical Association of America. He has published three books, written numerous articles for professional journals, and served as editor and consultant.

Credit by Examination in Historical Perspective

DONALD L. KREIDER

Great issues are measured by their ability to affect institutions, influence thinking, spark controversy, and define those watersheds in the affairs of the nation that lead to significant change. They have the potential to cause substantial advancement or dismal failure. By this measure credit by examination is such an issue. Few issues so thoroughly impinge on the traditions of our educational system; few have greater capability for bringing out diverging points of view; and few are so inevitable in terms of the social forces that gave them birth and therefore so insistently demand our attention.

The position of this paper is to affirm the social values and the educational legitimacy of credit by examination, at the same time recognizing its weaknesses and the problems it creates for college administrators and faculty.[1] High priority is given to the need for serious and informed consideration by all who are involved in, and concerned about, American education. To do otherwise is an unacceptable avoidance of our obligation as educators to provide leadership and to guide rather than to ignore the forces that strengthen the educational programs of our colleges and improve the educational opportunities of our citizens.

THE PRESENT SCOPE

In 1978 the College Board published an expanded and updated edition of the book *College Placement and Credit by Examination*. The revision, subtitled *1978 Guide to Institutional Policies*,

1. The author has benefited from previous conferences on this subject and is especially indebted to several thoughtful papers prepared by Jack N. Arbolino and John A. Valentine of the College Board. (See Selected Readings at the end of this chapter.)

provides a comprehensive listing of the institutions that honor, or grant credit or placement through, the College Board's Advanced Placement Program (APP), the College-Level Examination Program (CLEP), and the Achievement Tests of the Board's Admissions Testing Program. The information is based on a questionnaire that was mailed to all eligible institutions in January 1978.

Of the 1,541 colleges and universities responding to the questionnaire, approximately 1,100 indicated they have policies for granting some form of credit or advanced placement based on the AP Examinations in most of the disciplines covered. Approximately 850 institutions reported policies granting credit for various CLEP Subject Examinations; 850 to 900 institutions reported that they grant some credit for the CLEP General Examinations.

These facts, and the more detailed information in the book — broken down by geographic regions and states — indicate solid but uneven use of AP and CLEP examinations by United States colleges and universities. Patterns range from substantial use by some institutions to no use at all by others. Yet, although the AP and the CLEP candidates represent only a small fraction of all entering freshmen, the absolute numbers are now counted in the hundreds of thousands.

These two credit-by-examination programs taken together have thus become a significant factor for students as they plan which college or university to attend, and a significant factor also for institutions that face the prospect of increasing numbers of students who seek advanced placement or credit for some beginning courses. As a result, the spectrum of views and opinions about Advanced Placement and CLEP tests has broadened, and it is certain to promote interesting debate during the next few years.

THE ORIGINS

It is often supposed that credit by examination is a recent innovation. By some it is even identified with a computer-dominated society. But its roots extend far into the past. The University of London, for example, was established in 1836 as an examining body, not a teaching institution, and for more than 100 years it has been conferring degrees on so-called external candidates solely on the basis of their performance on examinations.

In the United States it has been a long-standing tradition at some universities to give students an opportunity to demonstrate their knowledge of material taught in certain courses on the basis of locally prepared examinations, thereby making it possible for them to receive credit for the courses without actually taking them. This practice has not generally affected many students, however, and the concept of credit by examination was essentially unrealized at a national level until the College Board launched its Advanced Placement Program and its College-Level Examination Program.

In a real sense, the idea of credit by examination had no relevance in this country until the end of the nineteenth century. Before then a college degree signified the completion of a rigid and universal curriculum, and the measurable quantity in a college education was the totality of the curriculum. There was no need, therefore, to attach credit to individual courses. In the late 1800s, however, Charles W. Eliot promoted at Harvard the radical new idea that students ought to have electives among their courses of study and, therefore, that individuals might be certified as "educated" even though they had not studied the same disciplines. In the twentieth century this inevitably led to the familiar college requirements now viewed as traditional — general education requirements to make certain that students have a common core of knowledge, distribution requirements to ensure breadth, language requirements to guarantee exposure to classical or modern languages, and concentration requirements to assure depth and focus. All these constructs made it essential to devise some form of "currency" with which to compare the depth, breadth, and rigor of dissimilar programs.

The currency is the course credit. Individual course credits have become building blocks with which an educational program is constructed and in terms of which progress toward its completion is measured. The idea has recently taken on yet more significance — indeed has become mandatory — in accommodating the mobility of today's population. It has become the basis for measuring equivalence between programs at different colleges and universities, permitting students — and credits — to transfer more freely between institutions.

Thus, while it is appropriate to keep in mind that the concept of course credit is relatively new, growing out of the needs of the knowledge explosion and of a highly mobile population in this century, we must recognize that the idea is defined more subjectively than objectively. In the minds of many educators a course credit not only measures achievement in accordance with a set syllabus; it also certifies that a certain process has taken place involving a teacher-student relationship, a classroom environment, peer support and competition, and grades.

Herein lies the difficulty in awarding credit for learning that takes place outside the traditional classroom setting. Herein also is the challenge to reexamine the meaning of individual courses in the educational whole. To what does a college degree attest? Does it, or should it, attest to the same thing for every individual, regardless of the program studied or the intended career? Does it certify what a person knows and can do? Or is it merely a statement about the quality and the quantity of educational experience, with the implicit conclusion that the person is therefore "educated" and prepared to be productive or creative on behalf of society or for himself or herself? These two possible interpretations are in conflict: measurement of achievement and competence on the one hand and assumption of growth, maturity, and creativity on the other. The main problem for educators has always been to keep such conflicting parts of the full educational picture in balance. It is important to prevent the instruments developed to measure competence and achievement from distorting those traditional educational values that are still useful. It is equally important to prevent adherence to an unformulated, and perhaps unmeasurable, concept of total education from smothering those innovations that are placing the benefits of further education within reach of a larger number of citizens. To permit these efforts to be stifled is to foster elitism to an extent that is unacceptable to American educators today.

The Origins of Advanced Placement

In attempting to recognize learning that has taken place outside the traditional college classroom, one can depart from that classroom in various stages. It is relatively easy to accept the fact that college credit might be awarded for courses taken elsewhere — in other colleges or in high schools. Here one can imagine that the nonmeasurable contributions of the classroom setting have had their effect and, therefore, that the student's success in learning can be tested on the basis of knowledge acquired in relation to a specific syllabus. This is the origin of the advanced placement movement that began a quarter of a century ago. It has been 25 years since the College Board launched its Advanced Placement Program, and the success of this program and its wide acceptance today often obscure the difficulty many educators had initially in believing that substantial college-level work could profitably and adequately be studied in high schools. Our memories are often fickle.

The Advanced Placement Program owes its start to two projects undertaken independently in the early 1950s with financial support provided by the Fund for the Advancement of Education of the Ford Foundation. The first project, initiated by the headmaster of Andover Academy, John M. Kemper, and known as the School and College Study of General Education, addressed the lack of articulation from school to college for many able, well-prepared students, which resulted in their studying essentially the same material twice. A committee composed of faculty members from three independent secondary schools (Andover, Exeter, Lawrenceville) and three universities (Harvard, Princeton, Yale) examined, and made recommendations regarding, steps that might be taken:

> What is needed is a set of achievement examinations in the major subjects taught in secondary schools which would enable the colleges supporting these examinations to give an entering student advanced placement in a subject like, let us say, chemistry; or credit for the prerequisite to majoring in history, for example, if that prerequisite happened to be a general course in American History; or even recognition of having the equivalent of a general education course in literature.[2]

2. "General Education in School and College: A Committee Report." Cambridge: Harvard University Press, 1953, pp. 118–119.

The second project set in place and in motion the basic components of the Advanced Placement Program. Conceived and directed by Gordon K. Chalmers, president of Kenyon College, and appropriately referred to as the Kenyon Plan, the project involved the cooperation of 12 liberal arts colleges, a number of secondary schools, and Educational Testing Service in the development of course outlines, the offering of courses based on these outlines, and the preparation of tests, also based on the outlines, which were administered to the first group of candidates from 18 schools in May 1954. In the fall of 1955, when responsibility for the program was formally transferred to the College Board, it became the national Advanced Placement Program as we know it today. The first administration of the examinations under College Board sponsorship took place in May 1956.

The idea of advanced placement is based on the fact that many young people in high schools are intellectually prepared to engage subject matter traditionally studied in the first college years. Although they may not be emotionally ready to move from the high school to the college environment, there is no reason to allow their intellectual momentum and curiosity to languish. It was also recognized that many high schools have both the desire and the resources to offer courses in some college-level subjects. The Advanced Placement Program was thus initiated to preserve an important national resource — the enthusiasm for learning of a significant number of our most talented young people.

The key to the Advanced Placement Program is the course syllabus, which serves as a framework for courses, a standard for achievement, a basis for testing, and a reference for colleges that wish to establish policies recognizing students' achievement. Such course descriptions, available in many subjects, are under continual review by panels of college and secondary teachers charged to monitor the program, to construct and evaluate its testing materials, and to communicate with schools and colleges throughout the country.

The growth of the Advanced Placement Program has been phenomenal — from a few hundred examinations when the program began to almost 140,000 examinations taken last year by a group of very able young people. For each examination a grade, on a 1-to-5 scale, is reported to colleges, and, as indicated earlier, some 1,700 colleges and universities now recognize these grades by awarding advanced placement, credit, or both. The success of the program is closely related to the high standards set for it by the College Board and implemented by the panels of teachers responsible for the course syllabi and the examinations themselves. The evolution of the course descriptions has been steady and predictable, and the technical quality and the consistency of the examinations have been carefully maintained by Educational Testing Service. But central to the program's wide acceptance is the involvement over the years of thousands of college and high school teachers in the preparation and grading of the examinations. The entire sociological enterprise has built important and healthy links between colleges and high schools and has led colleges and universities to recognize that AP students are well prepared and prized.

The Origins of CLEP

The success of the Advanced Placement Program paved the way for another, fundamental step away from the traditional college classroom—the recognition of learning that takes place completely outside the established school and college environment. This more radical departure came hand in hand with the need to provide educational opportunities for adults. It came in response to irresistible social pressure, summed up in the following statement by the American Council on Education's Commission on Educational Credit, urging postsecondary institutions to develop policies and procedures for measuring and awarding credit for learning attained outside their sponsorship:

> American society abounds in resources for learning at the postsecondary level. Public, private, and proprietary educational institutions exercise the central but not exclusive responsibility for instruction and learning. Associations, business, government, industry, the military, and unions sponsor

formal instruction. In addition, independent study and reading, work experiences, the mass media, and social interaction contribute to learning and competency.

Full and effective use of all educational resources is a worthy educational and social goal. Achieving this goal will depend to a large extent on providing equitable recognition for extra-institutional learning.

Educational credentials have a significant bearing on the economic, professional, and social status of the individual. Thus, social equity requires that equivalent learning, regardless of where and how it is achieved, be incorporated into the system of rewards for learning and competency.

Recognition encourages learning and contributes to pedagogical effectiveness. Teaching students what they already know is both stultifying to them and wasteful of educational and personal resources.

Behind this statement lies an impressive record of efforts by the American Council on Education, over a span of 30 years, to assist colleges in awarding credit for learning acquired in military and other noncollegiate settings, and also learning, however acquired, that is measured by examinations offered by the College Board through its College-Level Examination Program.

In 1966 the College Board introduced its College-Level Examination Program, funded substantially by both the Carnegie Corporation of New York and the College Board. The idea for such a program had been alive in the minds of a number of thoughtful educators for some time and had been promoted vigorously by John Gardner and other Carnegie officials. Educational Testing Service, under the leadership of Henry Chauncey, had moved to develop a set of comprehensive tests of college-level achievement, which became the basis for the first CLEP General Examinations.

The early years of CLEP were guided by the Council on College-Level Examinations of the College Board, a demonstrably distinguished group of educational leaders. A report to the College Board, urging the establishment of such a council, outlined the difficulties of initiating the program and predicted its unpopularity in some quarters. Yet, the social needs were seen as uncompromising, and it was viewed as essential to attempt a reconciliation between the requirements of social responsibility and academic detachment.

The Council on College-Level Examinations set long-range objectives for the new program. These were to provide instruments for measuring learning — no matter where it was acquired — that would be aimed especially at working men and women, ethnic and racial minorities, the disadvantaged, and the military. An additional objective was to gain acceptance for the concept through favorable college policies toward granting academic credit based on performance on the CLEP examinations.

Today CLEP offers two kinds of tests: General Examinations and Subject Examinations. For example, the General Examination in mathematics measures the basic mathematical ideas and methods considered essential for every college graduate, and there are tests in the subject areas of calculus, college algebra, algebra-trigonometry, trigonometry, and statistics. In all, some 50 tests cover dozens of disciplines.

It is, of course, a feature of American education that such courses are viewed as college-level work by some institutions but not by others. This is properly a local determination based on the institution's objectives and its students. When an institution does recognize study in these areas as college-level work for its own students and provides appropriate courses, it is likewise appropriate to establish policies of granting credit for CLEP examinations and similar testing instruments.

Unlike AP Examinations, CLEP tests are administered several times a year at more than 900 testing centers around the country. The tests are largely multiple-choice, although some have required or optional essays. The grades are reported on a nationally normed scale of 200 to 800; in addition the General Examinations report subscores for several areas. Although the national norms are intended to be useful to colleges and universities for interpreting individual scores on the examinations, the College Board recommends that local norming be carried out as institutions establish their own CLEP standards, thereby fairly measuring the desired knowledge, whether it is acquired in the classroom or gained elsewhere. Instead of suggesting that an institution apply the national norms, the College Board urges the determination of local norms with the full involvement of the faculty.

PROBLEMS

It is fair to say that most of the original objectives set for APP and CLEP have been met. Many people of all ages use the examinations as part of their own educational programs, and many colleges and universities award credit on the basis of the examinations, enabling these individuals to maintain continuous growth, minimize repetition, and progress more quickly to advanced study. In short, the programs facilitate a smooth transition into higher education for people with diverse preparation, capacities, interests, and ages.

But with success goes visibility, and with visibility go problems. First, there are problems of perception. Credit by examination is seen by some to erode the traditional teacher-student relationship. It is believed to replace the professional and personal judgment of quality provided by a classroom teacher with impersonal, nationally normed tests. It is thought to affect job security because students can bypass courses. It is assumed to influence curriculum development.

There is no denying that credit by examination has an impact in all these areas. Some of us have different degrees of concern, however, with regard to the somewhat vague notion of the teacher-student relationship, especially as it is implemented in none-too-perfect form in many classrooms across the country. We also differ in the level of confidence we have in the quality and consistency of evaluation given by many classroom teachers, especially in the environment of large lecture courses that are common in exactly the areas covered by CLEP examinations. We differ as to the very propriety of concerns about job security, as though educators have a right to tamper with the progress and the opportunities of citizens in order to fill classrooms. These issues are indeed apparent as a result of credit by examination, but we educators will continue to wonder whether they are positive or negative factors in education.

An immediate and serious problem, however, inevitably

follows the growth of a new idea such as credit by examination. The policies that serve as a base for implementing it are made by people who are far removed from the original objectives and principles and whose understanding of the subject matter and testing instruments is not adequate. Some state departments of education, for example, have required their state universities and colleges to award transfer credit based on CLEP General Examinations (1) without regard to whether the institution has courses in, or awards credit to its own students in, the area of knowledge to which the General Examination is directed; and (2) without taking into account the judgment of the institution's own faculty about the level and the needs of its students.

It is not uncommon in such cases for faculties and professional organizations to aim their anger and frustration at the General Examination itself rather than at the misguided political or bureaucratic decision that created the problem. One recent example involved the General Examination in mathematics and a decision of Florida's Department of Education. Fortunately a joint committee of the College Board and the Mathematical Association of America (Committee on Mutual Concerns) was able to deal with the problem. The General Examination, examined in detail by the mathematicians and the involved teachers, was judged to be perfectly appropriate *when administered in accordance with the College Board's own guidelines.* The State of Florida's requirement, however, was judged to be totally inappropriate because it failed to recognize local differences. The fortunate outcome was a joint statement by the College Board and the Mathematical Association of America to better inform educators about the purpose and proper uses of credit examinations. In particular, the joint statement underscored what has always been an intention of the CLEP program—that local faculty be involved in setting local norms for awarding credit on the basis of CLEP examinations.

Thus, real problems can and do arise, and strenuous efforts are needed to effect genuine solutions. But many of the critics of credit by examination, when listened to closely, seem to argue from less-than-noble premises. Criticizing the Advanced Placement Program as an elite program to serve the privileged few reflects an unfortunate point of view, endemic in American education. Such criticism has not retarded the growth of APP. Similarly, criticism that CLEP dilutes the quality of education because it enables students to avoid repetition both overestimates the impact of those beginning courses that present the corresponding material and underestimates the value of the three or more years of college or university education that remain even for those rare students who pass several CLEP examinations.

To criticize responsibly the various credit-by-examination programs, however, and to demand their continual improvement are important responsibilities for educators. This is precisely what the American Council on Education is doing through its Commission on Educational Credit—with the cooperation and encouragement of associations like the College Board to provide sharp reviews of the programs and tests. But it is hard to see what is contributed by detractors whose unstated agenda are not to provide constructive criticism but to return to simpler and less equitable times.

SUMMARY

The concept of credit by examination is here to stay. There remains only the question of how well we guide its further development and realize its potential. Problems of similar magnitude have been solved by the American educational system before; each time the system emerged stronger and with greater equity for all because educators have the capacity to accept a concept (even while criticizing it) and to see it through its growing pains. Credit by examination has deep historical roots, immediate and irresistible social relevance, and growing educational legitimacy. It is a catalyst for change in education and, while understandably arousing uncertainty and concern, has the potential to stimulate healthy and necessary debate over our national educational goals. We who support this concept believe it is not an overstatement to predict that from the perspective of the next century, credit by examination will be reckoned as an educational innovation on a level with the establishment of land-grant institutions and the elective curriculum.

SELECTED READINGS

Arbolino, Jack N. "The College-Level Examination Program: Another View." *Change,* April 1977.

Arbolino, Jack N. ". . . No Matter Where You Learned It." *The College Board Review,* No. 99, Spring 1976, pp. 13–20. A report on the first 10 years of CLEP.

Arbolino, Jack N. *A Report to the Trustees of the College Entrance Examination Board: The Council on College-Level Examinations.* New York: College Entrance Examination Board, September 1965.

College-Level Examination Program of the College Board. "A Bibliography of CLEP Research, 1972–1977." Mimeographed.

Stecher, Carl A. "CLEP and the Great Credit Giveaway." *Change,* March 1977.

Valentine, John A. "Learning: Questions of Standards and Credit." *New York University Educational Quarterly,* Vol. 8, No. 2, 1977, pp. 2–8.

2

Who gains most through credit by examination?

What makes professors uneasy about CLEP?

Calvin A. VanderWerf received a Ph.D. from Ohio State University in 1941. In addition to professional and consulting activities, he has been the author or coauthor of 100 articles, two textbooks, and a laboratory manual and a monograph in chemistry. Currently he is a professor of chemistry at the University of Florida.

Educational Significance of Credit by Examination: College Perspective

C. A. VANDERWERF

As a philosophical or a theoretical concept in the mind of the American taxpayer, credit by examination probably rates a shade above motherhood and only slightly below apple pie and Chevy Malibu. In theory we're for it. But when the concept is applied specifically to a course I am teaching, my reaction is markedly different. I believe with some fervor that something of significant value happens to a student in my classroom — something intangible, which cannot be measured. All of us who take pride in our teaching, I suppose, must believe that. This is one reason we are teachers.

And so it was that along with most other members of the faculty at the University of Florida, I viewed the State University System's adoption in 1972 of the most massive experiment in credit by examination conducted up to that time — and, I believe, up to the present time — with hostile alarm. Our overwhelming prediction, as faculty members, was that the results of the experiment would range from calamity to catastrophe.

Briefly, the State University Articulation Agreement between universities and community colleges decreed that CLEP credit could be awarded to students in the state institutions of higher learning on a standardized basis. The agreement provided that a maximum of 45 quarter hours of CLEP credit — 9 hours each of English, mathematics, humanities, and social sciences and $4\frac{1}{2}$ credits each in the biological and physical sciences — could be granted for satisfactory performance on the CLEP General Examinations, with the cutoff score set at the 50th percentile of the national sophomore norms for the CLEP examinations.

It was no problem for faculty members to react to the plan with both hostility and foreboding. In fact, the reaction came quite naturally. First, there was the usual, almost automatic, complaint that the plan had been hatched by meddlesome bureaucrats without adequate and representative faculty involvement or authority. Second, the scheme was an all-state, all-system one, with all the evils of uniformity and conformity that fact implies. Then, too, there was the strong suspicion that anti-intellectual legislators saw the program as a way to accelerate graduation, thus saving the state money by reducing the cost per student of a college education. Faculty members generally questioned the validity of granting college credit on the basis of scores from a general achievement examination. They believed that CLEP scores represented general abilities, not knowledge of specific course content. And the whole secondary school population (which would be involved) was not the group for whom the national CLEP program and the CLEP examinations had been devised.

Legitimate academic debate about the proper cutoff point could rage eternally. Expert faculty committees had studied the CLEP examinations assiduously and had found them generally comprehensive, fair, and of high and demanding quality both in content and in technical aspects. But there was no agreement on the cutoff point. Many faculty members declared that the 50th percentile was too low, and an even larger number maintained that it was too high. Nor was the welfare of the student entirely forgotten or ignored — although it was certainly not at the center of the CLEP controversy that gripped the state of Florida in 1972. Many faculty members thought the individual student who received CLEP credit on entrance into the university would, inevitably but unwittingly, be disadvantaged or handicapped intellectually and academically. There was fear that some enterprising, if not unscrupulous, administrators might seize the opportunity for a new recruiting device, with minimum regard for the welfare of the student.

Little wonder, then, that the majority of the faculty at our university viewed the impending CLEP program with more than concern and apprehension. The scorn that some members of the faculty felt for the plan was mitigated for me because, after all, three of the most humanely educated people I have ever known — my father, my father-in-law, and my oldest sister — earned graduate degrees in distinguished universities in this country without having attended a secondary school for a single day! Now, five years and several statewide and university studies and evaluations later, all of us are in a position to view CLEP's performance and potential with reduced passion and prejudice, and perhaps even with more concern for the welfare of the student and less for our own interests as teachers, administrators, legislators, parents, or simply taxpayers.

In summary, the results of the studies and evaluation conducted on our campus by a team of faculty and administrators indicated clearly that most of the apprehension and fears of the faculty members were unfounded.[1] Comparison of the CLEP group with the non-CLEP group of equal ability (as measured by the compulsory statewide Florida Twelfth Grade Test and Aptitude scores) revealed few differences in academic success. Briefly, the salient facts are these:

1. Grade point averages were virtually identical for the two groups.

2. A similar percentage of students in each group experienced academic problems.

3. The percentage of students in the non-CLEP group who withdrew from the university before graduation markedly exceeded the percentage in the CLEP group.

4. Forty-nine percent of the students with CLEP credit were graduated by the end of their fourth year at the university, compared with only 26 percent of the non-CLEP group.

5. Only 26 percent of the CLEP students were graduated in less than the usual four-year period, but the corresponding percentage of non-CLEP students was significantly lower (only 7 percent).

6. A striking majority of the CLEP students did not accelerate attainment of their degrees. Of this majority, some used their CLEP credit to enrich their program with a variety of advanced courses, others to reduce their course loads during certain quarters. Most of this group graduated with more than the minimum

1. Jeannine N. Webb, director of the University of Florida Office of Instructional Resources, who chaired our local study group and is far more expert in evaluation methods than I, is participating in this colloquium.

required number of hours. The credit hours earned in excess of the degree requirements indicate that although some CLEP credit was used, much of it was superfluous for graduation.

7. A significant number of the CLEP students who received their degrees in fewer than four years actually graduated earlier than their CLEP credit alone would have warranted. These students obviously carried credit overloads during some quarters, attended extra summer sessions, or both.

8. Apparently few students used CLEP credit to avoid taking courses in a particular area. Almost all CLEP students received CLEP credit in the field in which they eventually chose to major.

In the words of the University of Florida registrar: "Obviously our students who receive CLEP credit are in general a gifted and highly motivated group who use their CLEP credit wisely and flexibly to suit their own individual needs and purposes. There is no evidence that students suffer from participation in CLEP."

Also significant is that the faculty members who served on the CLEP study and evaluation task force, whatever their original skepticism or misgivings, now unanimously favor the program. The group did recommend, however, that for the University of Florida the minimum scores required for credit should be raised for the mathematics and physical science examinations and that the maximum CLEP credit granted in mathematics should be reduced from nine to four hours.

The results of these objective studies on our local campus and the corresponding statewide Florida State System studies, coupled with the imperative of preparing this paper, have forced me to reassess my own attitude toward credit by examination, or at least to reorder or reshuffle my prejudices and biases. Let me hasten to emphasize that I still hold the unshakable conviction that sitting in the class session of one of my own courses is a uniquely invaluable experience for which there can never be a completely adequate substitute. But I now have the temerity to ask myself whether, for a given student who has mastered the content of one of my courses, the possible benefits of receiving credit for that course could conceivably outweigh the value of the unique experience of taking it. This is a difficult admission for a teacher of 40 years' experience to make, especially to his fellow teachers. But the question is a fair and reasonable one, all the more so because, as an enthusiastic admirer and supporter of the Advanced Placement Program for the many years during which I have been associated with it, I have already accepted in principle the concept of college credit by examination.

Wherever I have been, I have actively recruited Advanced Placement students because I believe that, as a group, they represent a gifted and highly motivated — and a most fortunate — segment of our entering freshman class. However numerous and significant (and they are both numerous and significant) the benefits of an Advanced Placement program are to a secondary school, its teachers, parents, and the community, the major advantages and values come to the Advanced Placement students themselves — in challenge and motivation and in making possible an enriched and flexible collegiate academic program. Stated baldly, in those disciplines in which I am qualified to judge, a score of 5 or 4, and at times a 3, on an Advanced Placement Examination represents exceptional mastery of the intellectual content of the corresponding college course and an uncommonly rigorous preparation for subsequent courses. Objective studies have repeatedly verified this fact.

Substantial Advanced Placement credit is, I believe, an excellent predictor of success in college — so much so that even a prudent and conservative Dutchman would bet on it. Significant numbers of students who have earned Advanced Placement credit serve to leaven the entering class of any college or university. Some of these students may have advantages in admission to graduate and professional schools. The Advanced Placement Program has also contributed significantly to the all-important goal of bringing together high school and college teachers in mutual respect and cooperation and to improved articulation between high school and college curriculums in a wide variety of subject-matter areas.

Parenthetically, I recognize the widespread and understandable fear among teachers, discussed by Raymond Brokamp, that academically gifted students may bypass rigorous AP courses while in high school and be content with credit earned through CLEP. This is not an issue in Florida because CLEP credit is given only for the General Examinations, not the Subject Examinations. On a national scale I am confident that with the College Board's vigilance, which the continuing healthy concern of teachers will ensure, the two programs can be kept sufficiently distinctive in the populations and purposes they serve so that neither will contribute to the deterioration of the other.

Concerning the desirability and value of awarding CLEP credit to the adult, the mature, the nontraditional, the independent learner (the purpose for which the program was originally conceived), there appears to be relatively little controversy. To such learners the program has been a godsend. The process of evaluation, recognition, verification, and accreditation of nontraditional educational experience—in the library, the living room, or the company training and education program—has given hope, incentive, and a sense of worth to thousands. This is especially true of senior citizens, women whose education has been long interrupted, members of minority groups, and recent immigrants—all of whom often have a limited self-image as scholars or lack confidence in the possibility that their learning can be effective. To these groups, taking CLEP examinations for college credit must represent a most humane use of standardized examinations, one that eliminates needless and frustrating duplication and repetition and conserves talent, time, energy, and money. Certainly credit by examination constitutes an objective yardstick by which to assign credit for life experience. To the nation, CLEP for the adult learner represents a wise investment in human capital and a practical demonstration of the concept of diversity in education to which most of us give at least lip service. One long-range by-product of CLEP credit for learners in company educational programs may well be the development of better liaison between the academic community and business and industry.

The predicted explosions in lifelong learning and in widespread use of new technology, including computers, in teaching and learning have not yet occurred. The face of the future is difficult to discern, but many thoughtful futurists are predicting a revolution in learning that would enhance the significance and the societal value of credit by examination for the adult independent learner.

To return to the area of controversy: the use of CLEP examinations for the entering college freshman who is a high school graduate. In the words of one administrator: "Most of our faculty have learned to live with the Florida state CLEP credit-by-examination program as they would with benign illnesses — with an unconcerned tolerance." Others still regard all objective tests, norms, and exemptions with acute mistrust. College and university teachers — like all teachers — are extremely busy people. Teaching, research, service and committee assignments leave little time for any personal inspection and study of the validity of credit by examination for the traditional student. As a result, up to now, teachers have devoted little time to the question.

Increasingly I believe that the ultimate test of the program's validity must be what it does in and to the lives of students. Our registrar says that the CLEP program has been warmly received by almost all our CLEP students, to whose personal welfare it has made a notable contribution. Our director of admissions states that it has been of major assistance to many students in enhancing the articulation between the university and the high schools. Our director of preprofessional studies, a hard-bitten physicist, assures me that if there is proper guidance and counseling, CLEP credit can be of substantial benefit to the preprofessional student in making possible the design of a broad and flexible four-year curriculum, enriched with advanced courses.

Because it is essential, in evaluating any program, to hear from students directly, I met individually with scores of students who had received significant CLEP credit when they entered the university as freshmen. The following four case histories illustrate my findings:

• All her life Rosa has wanted to be a lawyer and is eager to be accepted into a distinguished law school. She plans to graduate after four full years of university work, with 27 hours of credit above the minimum required for graduation in her college. The CLEP credit she earned has made it possible for her to take several advanced courses as well as outside courses that otherwise she could not have included in her program. Rosa believes this will be a decided advantage when she takes the Law School Admissions Test.

• Betsy, a highly motivated medical student with clear career goals, wishes to become a specialist in pediatrics. She is a gifted student and an avid reader from a highly literate family; even as a college freshman she was largely self-educated, particularly in the humanities and social sciences. Betsy's CLEP credit enabled her to enter the special junior honors combined-degree medical program. She will soon graduate among the top five in her medical class, just seven years after entering the university as a freshman. She will use the year she saved through CLEP credits to spend an additional year in residency.

• Bob showed promise as a writer in high school. He hoped to be able to go to the university in his home town to major in creative writing. His mother is a widow, and, unfortunately, Bob needed to take a job to help support the family. Bob did take the CLEP General Examinations, however, and it was apparent that with the credits he earned he would be able to graduate in three years, even while working every summer. The extra credit provided precisely the financial margin he required to make a university degree a possibility. Bob carried a heavy credit load during three academic years, worked for a newspaper each summer, and graduated with honors. He is now an enterprising reporter for a Florida newspaper.

• Although Ivory planned to major in business, he believed that some business-related work experience might be essential to assure a position when he graduated. The CLEP credits he earned enabled him to carry a sufficiently reduced load during his junior and senior years at the university to work part-time in the office of a local industry, with no detriment to his academic performance. Ivory graduated in four years and, with solid recommendations from his part-time employer, was able to choose from among several job offers.

Most of the students in my study were self-reliant learners who used the CLEP credit they earned to enhance and enrich their university academic experience by taking diverse courses at advanced levels, not to abbreviate it. Of the minority who chose to shorten their college careers to fewer than the conventional four academic years, most expressed cogent and compelling reasons for doing so. Overall the students rated the CLEP credit-by-examination system as 10+ on a scale of 1 to 10.

The results of the universitywide studies of CLEP students at the University of Florida, as well as those of my smaller but more personal study, have caused me to examine my whole packet of beliefs about the unique and incomparable values derived from the now-traditional classroom experience. Are there truly values unattainable outside the college classroom? If so, how successfully do we convey these values to students or inculcate them into the lives of students? Just as one example, how successfully, through the classroom setting, do we inspire our students with a passion for lifelong learning? Are there alternative values of equal worth to society, and to students themselves, that would be fostered by more liberal credit-by-examination policies? These are significant and pertinent educational questions that, for the welfare of our students and the immediate future of higher education, we as teachers should address earnestly and vigorously. To ignore them is to default on our responsibility as educators. To inspect, to study, or even to try new systems of credit by examination is safe enough. After all, outside of the state of Florida, decisions about both the standards for credit by examination and the requirements that may or may not be satisfied by credit by examination usually are in the hands of the faculty of the individual institution, or of a department. If there is a danger of statewide control, it is better for the faculties to take the initiative in studying the question from within than to wait for orders from without.

The notion that nontraditional college-level education or independent study may be worthy of accreditation for all age groups is neither new nor revolutionary. For centuries and until quite recently, most learned men and women held that few educational experiences could be more liberating and humanizing than curling up with a truly great book. Perhaps—and I wince at the suggestion—we should return to the notion that learning, not teaching, is sacred. Perhaps here the result is more important than the process.

The moment has come, I sincerely believe, for the teaching fraternity across our nation to make a thorough and serious assessment of the concept of college credit by examination for high school seniors as well as for mature and independent learners. We may be entering an era in which the future of our democratic way of life throughout the world may well hinge on how strong and persuasive our incentives and our rewards are for all our citizens to learn — not just anytime and anywhere, but everywhere and at all times.

3

Why have teachers resisted national credit-by-examination programs?

Should CLEP exams be available to high school students?

Raymond J. Brokamp was graduated from the University of Cincinnati with a master of education in school administration. At present he is assistant superintendent of the department of curriculum and instruction of the Cincinnati Public Schools. He has been a mathematics teacher and a principal at a number of secondary schools.

Educational Aspects of Credit by Examination from the Secondary School Point of View

RAYMOND J. BROKAMP

Ibsen once said that the truth should be restated every 20 years. If that is true, the time is about right to reiterate the significance of advancing our talented pupils through challenging, rewarding, intellectual school experiences at the right pace and providing appropriate reward in the form of college credit and placement. The Advanced Placement Program became a reality, you see, in 1954, 25 years ago.

It has been my pleasure to have been associated with this significant movement from its inception. Indeed, it is fair to say that credit by examination and I have traveled parallel courses, arriving on the educational scene at the same time and experiencing one another from the outset. As a teacher, in the early years I struggled to convince myself and my colleagues that uniform standards had even a small chance in the diversity of American education. As a high school assistant principal and principal, I struggled to convince myself and my teachers that it was possible to elevate to college level some high school programs and thus bring about a change in the order. As a parent, I struggled to convince myself and my children that a contribution of time and money in the interest of high school college-level courses would produce an advantage to them. Now, as assistant superintendent of the Cincinnati Public School District, I am here to state the case. In sum, my response to these experiences is one of admiration for the concepts and for the processes.

Over these years I've often reflected on the struggle to initiate and maintain APP and, more recently, CLEP and have pondered the reasons for the enormous sacrifices of time and effort needed to generate national acceptance of educational concepts of such obvious advantage. If one assumes that approximately 15 percent of college-bound students can profit from APP, only 40 percent of those included in that conservative estimate are experiencing the advantage and only 20 percent of our high schools offer AP courses. As for the more youthful CLEP, the program is estimated to be at a small fraction of its full potential.

My conclusion is that the problem at the school level is chiefly related to provincial attitudes encountered at each step along the way. Indeed, Americans have prided themselves on the diversity of educational opportunity and have fashioned a national system characterized by diversity. Some men of academic exactitude would describe that system as no system at all — at least in the sense that it lacks national uniformity. We choose not to possess an absolute national school authority. Nor is there, as among some European nations, a uniform national body of schools with identical courses of study. Nor are there national standards, though interest is growing in that concept.

Illustrative of our heritage in this regard is an excerpt from a letter written by Benjamin Franklin in which he seems to approve an Indian attitude to the "white man's" education. He wrote: "The English Commissioners told the Indians that they had in their country a college for the instruction of youth, who were there taught various languages, arts, and sciences; . . . and said, if the Indians would accept the offer, the English would take half a dozen of their brightest lads, and bring them up in the best manner. The Indians, after consulting on the proposals, replied that it was remembered that some of their youths had formerly been educated at that college, but that it had been observed that for a long time after they returned to their friends, they were absolutely good for nothing; being neither acquainted with the true method of killing deer, catching beavers or surprising an enemy, [but] . . . if the English gentlemen would send a dozen or two of their children to Opondago, the Great Council would take care of their education, bring them up in what was really the best manner, and make men out of them."[1]

Franklin's letter characterizes the problem perfectly. We've been struggling with the issue since the beginning, weighing the

1. Thomas Woody, ed., *Educational Views of Benjamin Franklin*. New York: McGraw-Hill, 1931, pp. 110–111.

advantage of life-style and local needs against outside factors related to acceptable national goals and standards. The provincial outlook extends into our very system of schools and generates separation among preschools, primary grades, intermediate grades, middle schools, high schools, colleges, and graduate schools. Internally, we educators fail to fully integrate educational opportunities, programs, and teaching strategies among these various levels. Indeed, the really shocking statistics regarding the degree of acceptance and advancement of APP and CLEP are clear illustrations of the difficulty.

Nonetheless, credit by examination has established that it may be possible to have it both ways. We can now better reconcile local educational needs as expressed by the state, school district, or local school with the priority of developing youth to become intellectually what they are capable of becoming. This belief is reinforced in the light of the positive effect the APP has had on pupils and schools. In my experience, it has served to:

- Stimulate pupils
- Excite teachers
- Advance programs
- Improve libraries
- Articulate curriculum
- Save time and money
- Improve teaching
- Motivate the gifted
- Reward achievement
- Individualize education

Beyond these benefits, in the process of using Advanced Placement, we have generated a national consensus regarding acceptable standards and given perspective on the true intellectual capacities of youth—an achievement perhaps better described as an attack on the high school limits of knowing. We have, indeed, advanced the possibility that both the needs of our communities and their individuals may be well served. For once, gifted children can be reached in an environment that caters to their needs and successfully sidesteps characteristic, interminable debate and limited action regarding such snags as the definition of giftedness, identification of the gifted, and provision of suitable programs.

The beauty and success of both CLEP and AP is that the concept of credit by examination is basically simple. An acceptable (though often debatable) standard is established in a variety of disciplines, which provides the program focus. Debate and review involve questions that have proved to be difficult but manageable

—namely, what a college freshman should know. Thus, the more complex questions about the nature of giftedness in relation to the standards are properly left to those who deliver the program. At the school level many teachers I know have accepted the standards advanced and found them eminently reasonable and, more important, attainable by many pupils. They have been successful in assessing their pupils' qualities in relation to the standards and in devising educational systems and approaches to deliver the necessary knowledge and skills. In individual situations, everything from large-group instruction to individualized contract learning has proved successful. The key to success is an appropriate match among the standards advanced, the pupils served, and the educational tactics employed.

Thus, in fact, more clearly identifiable standards have arrived on the high school scene and have provided a national focus for learning activity as opposed to less clear, diverse, often lower-level efforts provided characteristically when the standards differ from school to school. Further, attainable college standards at the high school level have resulted in more elevated, attainable standards in grades 9 through 11, as well. Teachers at those levels are stimulated by the achievements and needs of AP teachers, with the result that learning has been advanced within all levels of schools where Advanced Placement courses have been instituted.

At this point it might be well to address a common problem related to lack of confidence in anyone else's standard. For example, there is a school-based fear that ETS specialists sit in isolation from the reality of college freshman academic life and, under such conditions, are prone to generate tests that have little to do with what actually is taught in a college and possess no relationship to the secondary school curriculum. These statements, taken from the College Board publication *College Placement and Credit by Examination*, should alleviate such fears. For APP, which relates to high school instructional programs and college standards, we find that "in every subject the course descriptions and the examination are the special responsibility of a development committee made up of secondary school and college teachers appointed by the College Board to overlapping terms."

For CLEP, which has no direct relation to instructional programs in secondary schools but is associated with college standards, we are told that "each examination is developed by a committee of college faculty working with test specialists at ETS. The
committee is responsible for preparing test specifications, developing and selecting test questions, reviewing statistical proper-
ties of the test, and preparing the description of the test for the
potential test takers."

Thus, in sum, the genius of these systems is that although
standards are jointly identified, program adaptation and experi-
mentation can occur freely at the local level without sanction,
prescription, or control from outside sources. Basic decisions
have been delegated to all interested parties. In APP, pupils and
parents volunteer themselves for the program prepared by each
local school faculty. College faculties review the qualifications of
the pupil and render an independent decision regarding placement and credit. In this complex joining of disparate elements, the
glue is the standard set cooperatively by professional participants
at various levels.

In my view, secondary teachers and administrators who have
failed to embrace these programs are likely to have mispercep-
tions regarding the following:
1. Capacity of talented persons for advanced work
2. Availability of talented students
3. Pupils and their motivation
4. Real possibility of gaining college credit
5. Possibility of organizing instruction at school level
6. Availability of qualified secondary teachers
7. Academic pressure
8. Teaching-for-tests principle

The result of these and other anxieties is unnecessary fear of failure and lack of initiative. To those with such concerns, I offer the
thought that every one of these issues was attacked successfully
last year in over 4,300 high schools presenting AP Examination
candidates and nearly 2,000 colleges accepting AP and CLEP candidates. Pogo's famous assertion applies here, as on other fronts:
"We have met the enemy and he is us." We have no one to blame

for withholding educational advantage for our talented youth but those of us in command of the levers that will release the appropriate opportunity.

As with any human system, problems remain that need continual attention. Standards will always be at issue, and evident strategies will have to be pursued to adjust them appropriately. The challenge is to demonstrate continually the dynamic nature of the program and to reveal clearly the open nature of investigation.

A prevailing view among secondary educators is that CLEP is academically less challenging than APP and that this condition places rigorous high school programs in jeopardy. Such thinking generates school worry that CLEP will contribute to the flight of talented students from high school to college without the advantage of the senior high school year. In fact, these fears have apparently not been realized in the Cincinnati area or in other parts of the country of which I am aware. The concern is strong, however, and misunderstanding runs deep. Steps must be taken continually to demonstrate the qualities of both CLEP and APP and to assert that each serves particular college clienteles well.

The Board's publication *CLEP General and Subject Examinations* states: "Anyone may take CLEP tests to demonstrate college-level competency, no matter where or how this knowledge was acquired." That concept is applied in the following way at one prominent university: "High school students interested in obtaining EM credit (by exam) through the CLEP program may find it convenient to take such examinations while in high school, and they are encouraged to do so." In my view arrangements like this influence academically capable high school students to bypass rigorous AP courses in favor of taking CLEP tests before they complete the senior year. Indeed, CLEP examinations are normed against satisfactory achievement in a generality of American colleges, but AP Examination standards are based on satisfactory achievement at selective colleges. Bright students will not forever remain unaware that a strong possibility exists at many colleges for them to obtain greater credit with less work if they pursue CLEP tests. The conclusion would be unfortunate because of the enormous AP enrichment opportunities such students would miss.

As indicated before, my experience suggests that relatively few high school students are taking the CLEP route to college credit, compared with those who take AP Examinations. The primary reason may be that high school counselors are in part unaware of such arrangements, and when they are aware, they may be unwilling to promote such questionable tactics.

I suggest the College Board statement quoted above be changed to: "Anyone *no longer in high school* may take CLEP tests to demonstrate college-level competency, no matter where or how this knowledge was acquired." In short, the amount of mistrust of CLEP being generated at present at the school level is not worth the highly questionable advantage some colleges and the College Board apparently attribute to global eligibility for CLEP tests.

The reluctance of many colleges to grant degree credit is particularly sad and mystifying. Follow-up studies confirm that AP and CLEP students do as well as, or better than, their peers in subsequent college courses. Further, such studies also confirm that there is a higher retention rate among such students. My advice to graduating high school AP seniors is to list colleges capable of meeting their educational objectives and then to evaluate the amount of credit available to them in each institution for college-level work already attained. You may be assured that hundreds of such decisions, of which I am personally aware, have been made in favor of colleges willing to acknowledge achievement, however it has been brought about. It is gratifying that hundreds of colleges now grant sophomore standing to eligible students. In the interest of our students and programs, hundreds more need to be added to the growing list.

The reality of our condition is that high school teachers and administrators are depending on college colleagues to validate high school work fairly by providing immediate access to advanced college work with appropriate credit. We at the school level are dealing with thousands of teenagers who are impressed with the example of college decisions in this area and are willing to work unbelievably hard if the reward merits the necessary sacrifices. In my opinion, colleges and universities that cast doubt on APP and CLEP by withholding credit and placement to qualified students are greatly and unnecessarily limiting the number of high school pupils who take advantage of the opportunity.

Of similar concern is the reality that some colleges fail to make clear what their policies are in regard to APP and CLEP. Thus, students are surprised and frustrated when anticipated credit is not made available, with the result that the integrity both of high school and of college programs is doubted. College officials must realize they are often dealing with inexperienced, immature senior high school students who, unfortunately, may assume that sacrifice of time and energy for excellence in college-level high school courses will be acknowledged by credit at the collegiate level. Such students are not inclined to read between the lines, and unless given very careful guidance, they will enroll in one college when another is clearly to their advantage.

Over the years we've all observed that the major advances in social, scientific, economic, and religious thought come from our exceptionally knowledgeable and gifted citizens. Indeed, there is no need for apology or excuse, and every reason for pride and perseverance in discovering exceptional gifts and providing an outstanding educational environment for this needy group.

Plato said, "What is honored in a country will be cultivated there." Robert Louis Stevenson captured what might best be honored when he stated: "To be what we are, and to become what we are capable of becoming, is the only end of life."

The AP and CLEP examinations make possible an appropriate ascent toward the extent of our intellectual capacity, while rewarding those who have the will to make the extra effort. The system works! I strongly recommend it to you.

Following his presentation of the paper, Raymond Brokamp led a discussion of some of the issues raised. The questions, posed by members of the audience, were answered first by Mr. Brokamp. Additional responses and comments were made by other colloquium participants. Highlights are given here in edited form.

Question: What is the justification for the two sets of norms you spoke of for the two examination programs?

Response: As I understand it, each program serves a particular clientele. The Advanced Placement Program enrolls large numbers of youngsters who are going to colleges with selective admissions criteria, and therefore youngsters who successfully complete AP Examinations should be able to participate successfully in those colleges — as opposed to the CLEP program, which serves a larger group of colleges.

Another response: One of the purposes of the Advanced Placement Program is to provide for able high school students, through the work of subject-matter committees, curricular goals and tests that will open doors at the colleges to which they are most likely to proceed. A broader range of colleges (at the same time with a more specific college purpose) likes to use CLEP because it helps them identify among the incoming students those youngsters or oldsters who have already learned, one way or another, some of the subject matter taught at that college. This is a little like the corpuscular theory of light: A phenomenon can be looked at from one point of view or another. In the world we live in, both of these things are going on at once.

Another response: To address the question of two sets of norms: While it's true that the programs can serve different kinds of students who are going to attend a variety of types of institutions, there's also a fundamental difference in the way in which the scoring is set up; Ernest Kimmel deals with this extensively in his paper, which we are to discuss later.

In brief, the Advanced Placement Program's 1-to-5 scale represents an absolute judgment by professionals (the teachers), who are competent in the body of knowledge being tested. In that sense APP does not have a normative-based scale, but a scale that expresses a grade of 1 through 5 [not a score] in terms of competence as judged by teachers.

The CLEP program has a basically different approach. It uses the 200-to-800 College Board score scale, with scores along the scale based on the performance of what we call a reference group of students from a cross section of colleges. We've had increasing difficulty, incidentally, in getting colleges to cooperate in the testing this requires. We are now moving to supplement such reference-group data with faculty judgments about performance on the examinations that represents competence at the college level. We've been convening faculty panels to tell us what kinds of scores in the 200-to-800 range they think reflect reasonable levels of competence, and we hope shortly to provide information of this sort to supplement the scores on the CLEP scale.

Question [from a professor]: I have a question about your remarks on when the CLEP test should be taken. Our university does offer some CLEP credit. We have a preorientation program in the summertime, and we recommend that students take CLEP tests in the spring of their senior year so that the results will be known before they come for advisement. Is there any objection to that?

Response: No, I see no problem with testing in the spring of a youngster's senior year. The problem, as I see it, is that some colleges are willing to have the testing precede the senior year. Youngsters so tested, if successful, might think twice about pursuing a rigorous course of study in their senior year. But at the time you specify, the die has been cast as far as choosing to take Advanced Placement courses is concerned, and the risks to the learning process are reduced.

Comment: I'm sorry to hear you retreat a bit from the proposal in your paper that the College Board should specify that no one in high school may take CLEP. I think that's a very sound suggestion. The CLEP tests are less expensive than the AP Examinations, and if the student is faced in May with the decision of whether to take CLEP or AP, economics—let alone academic standards—might dictate that CLEP is the more reasonable choice. I, for one, would like to endorse your proposal.

Another comment: I don't fully understand the logic you used in developing the case against taking CLEP tests at, say, the end of the junior year in high school. How could that threaten the guidance for secondary school programs? It seems to me that if students were to take CLEP or AP after their junior year in high school and prove they could obtain advanced standing at some university in that subject area, it is to the students' benefit to know that, so they could expand the areas in which they might study in the senior year in high school. And it could have the effect of strengthening some of the Advanced Placement courses. If, on the basis of the CLEP mathematics test, for example, students appear ready for advanced standing, perhaps they could take an Advanced Placement course in some other area. If a CLEP test reveals they are not ready, it seems as though it could be a valuable counseling guide and really doesn't represent a threat to them.

Response: I think there is some merit in your comment. It assumes, however, that the curriculum at the high school level is very broad and that youngsters have equally profitable academic opportunities in a wide range of areas. The reality is that rigorous college-level courses at the high school level are rather scarce. Most schools have one, two, or a few, if any, Advanced Placement courses to offer. Therefore, if youngsters take the CLEP mathematics test at the end of the junior year, do exceedingly well on it, and have ahead of them in high school a single opportunity in APP, possibly mathematics, I think we have adversely affected the students' opportunities in the field of mathematics — assuming that they choose *not* to proceed through the more rigorous courses. In high schools where youngsters have limitless opportunities [for college-level courses], the point you make is valid. But, as I said, only about 20 percent of the high schools have Advanced Placement courses at all, much less the full range of 24 courses.

Comment [from a student]: I believe that it's often beneficial to take a CLEP examination after your junior year if you're dealing with that subject matter as a junior, whereas if you wait another year, you're probably going to score worse.

Response: I think that is a good statement. But the question is the effect CLEP may eventually have on APP at the high school level. I believe there is danger of the abandonment of Advanced Placement courses in schools. I would like to maintain the Advanced Placement Program and make certain that CLEP is administered only at the end of the high school years.

Comment: I have a schizophrenic academic career. I spent 10 years at Harvard running the Advanced Placement Program. The last two years I've been dean of a university that has adult students and is very heavy on CLEP. So I've had an opportunity to observe the results of both programs. Also, I have a healthy regard for students' ability to seek out among the cornucopia of options presented to them those that they consider most appropriate to their life careers. At Harvard we had 1,600 freshmen, 400 of whom were eligible for sophomore standing, and every year fewer elected to take that option. Of those who took it, fewer graduated in three years. They were more likely to explore the greater options possible within the four years: perhaps two degrees; some pregraduate degree while in the nurture situation, rather than to be thrown immediately into the law, medical, business, or graduate schools of education. I never really understood why that was happening, and it was always a great concern because the Advanced Placement Program was a wonderful recruiting technique for the university.

Now, in a university whose students are generally four or five years older [than the Harvard students], I find they are not so interested in more options within the four-year period. Very few will go immediately to graduate school, although they may eventually go to graduate school in a weekend or an evening format. For them the CLEP opportunity is very important because it shunts aside a lot of what they believe are the initial barriers to the four-year experience — those things that we introduce to make sure that people get over the hurdles. They usually have fewer resources; they have other obligations, too, and they think that getting those out of the way will permit them to get through more quickly. So, I don't necessarily see that conflict the way I used to see it. I think there's a philosophical or a student-oriented background to these programs that hasn't necessarily emerged yet from some of the comments made here about when the programs are given and to which populations they are given.

Question: What is the advantage to the student of APP over dual enrollment at a nearby college [while the student is still in high school]?

Response: There are very few Cincinnati institutions of higher education that offer the dual enrollment opportunities. Advanced Placement has been well established almost from the outset, and, as a result, it prevails. Therefore, the kind of program you're asking about, which might be very constructive, simply hasn't emerged to any degree in Cincinnati.

Comment: I'm distressed that you're viewing APP and CLEP as adversaries, or at least as competitors. I view them more as kissing cousins.

Response: It's the question of how they are administered, in my opinion, that will determine how cordial that kissing relationship turns out to be.

Question: I'm wondering if it makes any difference whether a high school student demonstrates competence in calculus or college algebra or literature in APP or CLEP? Why restrict it to age? We're interested in the student and not the institution.

Response: Keep in mind my premise that the standards of the examinations in some of the areas common to APP and CLEP are different. Given that reality, the complications we've been discussing could emerge and in some cases have emerged. If the examinations are precisely the same, the point you make is sustained; but as long as the standards vary, the issue will remain.

What facts help to evaluate APP and CLEP?

Who should be involved, and how?

Franklin Lane McKean is currently dean of student affairs and services at the University of Utah, where he received a master of science in educational psychology. Past positions at the university include dean of admissions and registration and dean of academic advising. He is affiliated with several professional organizations, including the National Association of Collegiate Admissions Counselors, the American Association of Higher Education, and the Utah Personnel and Guidance Association. He is a retired major general in the United States Army Reserve.

Development of Sound Institutional Policies of Credit by Examination

FRANKLIN L. McKEAN

The passage of credit by examination from an acceptable theoretical model to a practical one is marked by pitfalls that many administrators are either wise to ignore or, in their ignorance, fortunate to avoid without fatal consequences.

As a philosophy, credit by examination has been part of higher education for many years. Its factual origin is probably lost in the minutiae of faculty and administrative council minutes; yet it is cited as a policy, if not a practice, in most institutional publications. There seems to be an inherent "good" in allowing bright and strongly motivated, yet traditionally oriented, individuals to demonstrate what has been learned outside the formal context of the classroom. Faculties are always pleased to evaluate nontraditional student learning experiences on a limited basis. Departments point with pride to their "unique" students who have demonstrated accelerated learning or special knowledge in a self-developed environment—for example, the bright youngster who at age 15 is a mathematical whiz or the oldster who comes back to complete a baccalaureate with waivers in accounting because that happens to be his or her profession. But if credit by examination becomes significant, either when students are offered attractive alternatives for gaining college credit without the quid pro quo of time or money spent, or when energetic high school programmers and others develop programs that support credit by examination, the concern is real and practical.

The reasons are apparent. There are a loss of student credit hours, uncollected tuition because of shortened programs, and for some a genuine concern about the quality of the program offered. The impact these factors may have on the initial decision of an institution to accept credit by examination cannot be ignored, but what follows are some suggested ways to avoid the fatal traps, errors, and deterrents to an effective credit-by-examination program if a significantly strong group of faculty and administrators in an institution of higher education want it to succeed.

As mentioned, most institutions have traditionally indicated, in their catalog or other official publications, their commitment to credit by examination. Typically, however, there has been a significant disparity between commitment and practice. This paper addresses the bridging of that gap.

THE ESSENTIALS OF ACCEPTANCE

The first and basic element in the development of a credit-by-examination program is the personal commitment of a significant individual or a group of individuals, including faculty and administrators, who believe it is a legitimate, academically acceptable, and reasonable alternative method of offering college credit.

Once this committed group has emerged, a second essential must be present. The committed group must develop and seek acceptance of a practical institutional philosophy regarding credit by examination. (The term "practical" may be defined as the possibility that such a program will allow students in the top half of their group to qualify for credit.)

In addition to the key individual or group suggested above, whether they are deans, the president, or committee chairpersons, the process requires the full involvement of the institution's thinkers and movers. Such contributors could include, but need not be limited to, the academic vice president, the dean of liberal or general education, the dean of the arts and sciences colleges, and other key faculty and faculty committees.

Depending on the type of institutional governance, it is necessary to involve directly the president or the chief administrative officer in some timely and ongoing fashion. This ensures that the officer is aware of the program and can, at strategic times, offer advice and continuing support. The impact that significant amounts of credit earned by examination may have on the institution needs to be assessed. The chief administrative officer should be kept apprised in as much detail as possible of the total impact in matters of full-time equivalence, student credit hours, and income earned or lost. This evaluation process ought to include consideration of the effect of credit by examination on recruiting, retention, number of quarters or semesters an individual spends as a traditional student in earning a baccalaureate degree, total income from tuition versus total income lost by awarding credit by examination, shifts in program strength (for example, offering substantial amounts of liberal education by examination rather than through course involvement). The acceptance of credit earned by examination should be evaluated as an academically legitimate means of partially satisfying baccalaureate degree requirements. For the beginners these questions have no immediate answer because of the lack of data, and for many other institutions computer-assisted modeling programs may not be available. To do or not to do becomes a risk administrators are paid to take.

Rather than getting mired in trying to arrive at answers before a basic credit-by-examination policy is articulated, the institution, for its own purposes, should make a decision on the appropriateness of credit by examination. The growing volume of research, while not conclusive in support or rejection of the program, can provide some comfort to those who make the decision. Ten years subsequent to the acceptance of credit by examination through the College-Level Examination Program (CLEP) and the Advanced Placement Program (APP) and the resulting generation of significant hours of examination credit, attempts are still being made to evaluate the economic impact. (See *The Economic Impact of Credit by Examination Policies and Practices,* John R. Valley, editor, published by Educational Testing Service, 1978.)

Use of Data to Support Decision Making

Whether the important concerns of loss of income and student credit hours can be ignored in the early stages of the institutional policymaking process is a question that requires some courage on the part of the recommending committee. Many programs can effectively be blocked, sidetracked, or submerged by "very good questions" for which, in many instances, there are no answers, simply because the data are not available. Any question asked of credit by examination should be asked of typical programming.

For example, if we expect people who pass CLEP at the 30th percentile to be able to write an acceptable essay, should we expect the same of people who get a D or a C in a beginning English composition class? Also, the criteria of judgment should be the same. The basic question of whether credit by examination is a useful means of assessing educational achievement needs to be considered as a fundamental philosophical tenet of the institution. The key question is: If credit by examination is a legitimate means of measuring and accepting atypical educational accomplishments, can this method assume an equally valid position parallel with the other acceptable and institutionally approved measures of these educational accomplishments? If credit by examination appears to be for the common good, but its acceptance raises other problems such as faculty load and loss of student credit hours, these problems should be examined outside the context of the program. If the final commitment of the institutional study group is to support credit by examination as an acceptable basis for recognizing educational accomplishment, the position should be freed from the obfuscating practice of raising "what ifs," the professional rhetoric that is often based on unenlightened vested interest or general institutional inertia.

FOLLOWING ACCEPTANCE—THEN WHAT?

Once the acceptance of credit by examination as an institutional policy is clear, the more important consequences of the program should be examined and made apparent to all.

Will credit by examination satisfy more than general, or liberal, credit hour requirements for the baccalaureate degree? Can the liberal, or general, education requirements be satisfied by tests such as the General Examinations of the College-Level Examination Program? The dean or the director of the liberal education program and the supporting committee can make this assessment. If the group decides that the credit-by-examination process will not satisfy liberal education program requirements or measure the end result of a liberal education, little further productive dialog is possible unless the governing body of the institution overrides the recommendation. In my opinion, however, there is not a strong likelihood that vigorous faculty opposition to the satisfaction of liberal education program requirements by examination would bring about such an overriding regulation.

Other individual faculty members and academic departments for whom subject-matter examinations are a concern must be fully involved in the dialog, particularly as it relates to the validity of the tests. The instruments must be reviewed and evaluated not only by the faculty who are subject-matter experts, but also by testing and test construction experts. A thorough technical review of the test — its validation process, norming populations, and other pertinent technical data — should be made apparent and available for examination by all, whether or not it is completely understood. Bringing an examination on campus that hasn't been through the internal institutional review process is tantamount to failure.

The question of what a program such as credit by examination will do for higher education in general or for the particular education (community college, continuing education, and so forth) in which the institution is involved must be considered. Should access to this model of learning evaluation be limited to certain populations, such as middle-aged adults, or to the student public in general? Are there reasons for limitations either by age or by previous school or enrollment status? Would opening up this process increase access to higher education? Can it encourage a new population such as atypical (by age) students who may, based on information acquired, be able to enter a baccalaureate program mid-course and complete the process without the traditional four-year involvement? Might this new population increase enrollments? Could such an increase be offset by students who complete their work within a shorter period of time?

These are the nuts-and-bolts questions the administration and the supportive committees must be ready to answer as the process is reviewed by the university's governing body, whether it is an administrative council or a faculty senate.

Presentation to the ultimate governing body for approval and acceptance must have support from the three elements of authority typical of higher education institutions. These are, first, the administration — the president, vice presidents, provosts, or others who occupy that position; second, the collegial groups — the faculty committees, deans, and other representatives of reviewing and policymaking bodies; third, the professional members of the staff—the management experts, education specialists, and others who provide the analytical data and without whose support the development of a program acceptable to the governance committees, whether they are faculty, senate, or college councils, is not possible.

In state or regional systems, once the governing body of the system approves credit by examination, it must be accepted by all member institutions. Mobility of the student within a system is vital, and manipulation of the program's credits—for whatever purpose—can be extremely detrimental not only to the student but to the institution.

Research Support

While the articulation and acceptance of an institutionwide credit-by-examination policy is the first and most important step, a close follow-up is an effective research base. Norming data are essential, whether these data are derived from local populations as part of a test development program or from national studies of larger and more heterogeneous populations. The institution must accept these data (if they are demonstrably valid) and their meaning, and then develop a position that takes the data into account. Those groups who oppose credit by examination or who are not sophisticated in formal test construction theory seem to have a natural reluctance to trust data. Whether they can be trained to accept data-based conclusions may be questionable, but data should be relied on.

Institutional reviewers must be ready to allow the inclusion of a safety factor in setting credit levels based on these norms. The procedure should not become a point of contention unless the proposed credit levels negate the program. These differences can be resolved through various arbitration and decision-making techniques and can eventually be modified to a level that is acceptable to faculty and students.

Program Transferability

As mentioned above, attempts should be made to develop local or national norming data. These data may facilitate the acceptance and transfer of credit by examination. When a state system allows direct transfer within the system, students are not penalized by their involvement in a credit-by-examination program that is not accepted by other system-related institutions. Administrators within a state system or other consortia should vigorously seek the cooperation of other institutions in developing a common program for transferring these credits. The very concept of credit by examination suggests a broadened opportunity base for the atypical student.

National organizations such as Educational Testing Service, the College Board, and others involved in evaluating the program, developing new norms, modifying the test instruments themselves, and maintaining a responsive stance to suggestions from the user institutions can be of great service to a school seeking to develop a credit-by-examination program. These services will, in many ways, soften the call for a constant reevaluation that seems to be a part of any credit-by-examination program. It is an unfortunate corollary that when environments change—for example, when student enrollments drop for completely unrelated reasons—credit by examination is scrutinized again by some academicians who question whether anyone can learn outside the institutional environment. This "carousel" effect, as reported by Baldridge and Teal, keeps credit-by-examination users and proponents responsive to the need for constantly supporting the production of academically sound and legitimate processes and studies.[1]

The credit-by-examination program must have stability if it is to survive in today's educational environment. As suggested earlier, the state boards of regents or members of regional governance bodies should adopt a systemwide policy pertaining to credit by examination. This policy, whether it is in terms of fiat or regulation, should be simple and understood by all institutions in the system so that the program may readily be defended from those who would change it. Such an overall governance policy is invaluable in support of the systemwide studies that should be part of the total program.

The involvement of secondary schools in understanding a

---

1. J. V. Baldridge and T. E. Deal, *Managing Change in Educational Organizations.* Berkeley: McCutchan, 1978.

credit-by-examination program cannot be overlooked. The participation in the College-Level Examination Program by younger students just out of high school suggests some interesting relationships that are not entirely unexpected. The Advanced Placement Program, which has been a widely accepted high school–oriented activity for many years, has the advantage of being easily understood. A student who participates in Advanced Placement not only takes a final examination but is also involved in a course experience. While this activity is generally accepted as credit by examination, it closely parallels the traditional learning process.

The University of Utah, for example, distinguishes clearly between credit earned by APP and that earned by CLEP. The Advanced Placement Program as followed by the major high schools in the area served by the university is active in sponsoring a faculty-directed classroom experience. The subject matter is well defined and the level of performance measured by well-accepted instruments. As a consequence, AP credit is accepted as college transfer work within the discipline represented. The College-Level Examination Program and other non-course-related examinations, on the other hand, challenge the traditional understanding of, and raise questions concerning, the legitimacy of the high school effort to teach concepts and provide information that can be translated into college credit.

The data base for this concern needs to be examined. High school students who receive AP and CLEP credit do not represent the norm. These atypical students are only a segment of the diverse high school population. To expect everyone to learn at the same rate or intensity, or to retain information or to advance or to mature at the same rate is one of those obvious errors that should not have to be mentioned. Yet, somehow, we forget this and expect all high school students to look very much alike when they begin college as entering freshmen. In turn, they are expected to take about four years to complete the baccalaureate degree. Fortunately, we are able to remind ourselves of the truism that people grow and learn differently. If this were not so, most of us would live a fairly boring existence because we could learn to predict behavior accurately and thus lose all challenge.

It is not unusual for a bright, strongly motivated high school student to start college with a year of credit given through APP, CLEP, or some other acceptable credit-by-examination experience. This does not necessarily mean that the fourth year of high school should be eliminated for these students simply because of a different rate of motivation and learning. It does suggest that for some students there is no necessity to repeat educational programs that have been adequately covered in the student's secondary school experience. Mutual understanding, support, and feedback between the two major elements of the education system, college and high school, need to be part of the evaluation process.

Disclosure of the Programs

The study and eventual announcement of an institutional or systemwide credit-by-examination policy should be handled carefully. Just as the original decision is made to accept it as an educational concept with philosophical validity, without reference to the possible mechanical impacts on the system, the temptation to exploit certain inherent advantages such as recruiting and retention should be avoided.

Information about credit by examination should be made available by the usual means, such as publication of the policy in the university catalog. Specific low-key informational brochures relative to the program, as well as evaluation data describing the credit transferability and educational program requirements it might meet, should also be published in a dignified format.

Credit by examination is not and should not be the answer to the economic and curricular ills of an institution. Its validity and acceptability should be based on what it can do for the student by recognizing the existence of an atypical learning experience.

Recording Credit by Examination

It is important to establish a simple internal recording and processing procedure. The evaluation and subsequent recognition of credit by examination should be related to an easily understood equivalent of credit-hour or program completion. The subject-matter examinations are simpler to evaluate and record than are

CLEP General Examinations. Consequently, general examinations should be related to programs rather than to particular subjects.

Registrars and admissions evaluators should be certain that the meaning of the transcript or record is clear. The evaluations should transmit data in a manner congruent with the policies developed by the institution and its governing bodies.

The institution should provide testing centers that not only provide the testing opportunity but also give full information about the accessibility of such credit or its transferability among similar institutions. Full disclosure of the institution's policy on credit, scores, and transferability must be part of the original commitment.

Research Base

An institution committed to credit by examination will, if the program is to be effective, develop an effective support system. Such a system must include the involvement of an academic division such as educational psychology, the psychology department, or the institutional research office. These divisions can support the necessary testing service agency and can provide for gathering the data needed to evaluate the program.

The research function should demand the same rigor that general social science research requires. The "N of one study," with the dean's daughter as the subject, seems to be insufficient data. If someone's son said the test was too easy—hence we should stop testing—the same ought to hold for a class that someone reported was too easy.

Off-Campus Relations

Participants in the university's off-campus relations activity, whether it is a high school or junior college relations program or a community service bureau, should be completely familiar with the credit-by-examination policies and programs. High school students and other individuals interested in the program should be fully apprised of both the benefits and the limitations. Because institutional policies may vary considerably from one area to another, the evaluation and information processes must include facts about what is acceptable at institutions to which the student might be applying or transferring.

The institutional advising and counseling agencies must also be fully aware of the program as they talk with students about course selection, career choices, individual curriculum planning, and other kinds of decision making. Credit by examination is typically not the sole or the primary method of meeting the baccalaureate degree requirements — as college catalogs will explain.

The nuances of the program, the implications of its acceptance by other institutions as part of the undergraduate program, how the program is viewed by professional graduate schools — all must be understood and properly communicated in counseling or advising. The decisions the student makes in using the program must be part of the total program development.

CONCLUSION

Much of the "advice" given above regarding credit-by-examination program development is based on personal experience.[2] Whether it is applicable in other circumstances or within other institutions is problematical. What is important is that if a study is initiated to review the question of credit by examination and if the program is accepted, a vigorous approach must be taken. The concerned, supportive faculty and administrators must concentrate their personal and combined efforts to make it work. If the program is identified as a worthy and legitimate means of recognizing differences among students and allowing them to take advantage of these differences, it is vital that the program be pushed, with full awareness of the past histories and the future complications and impacts. The genius of higher education appears to be in its ability not only to initiate educational programs but to respond to change stimulated by external forces. Credit by examination may be such a catalytic agent.

2. The credit-by-examination program at the University of Utah was reviewed by a university faculty committee in 1972, four years after the program's adoption. The faculty report is reprinted in its entirety as Appendix 1 of this paper.

If the basic question is whether credit by examination is worthwhile, and if the answer is yes and the reasons are educationally defensible and compatible with the institutional mission, then all honest effort ought to be made to change credit-by-examination theory into practice.

Appendix 1:
Report on the College-Level Examination Program to the University Senate
by
The Committee on Credits and Admissions
April 24, 1972

INTRODUCTION

The College-Level Examination Program (CLEP) General Examinations were first used to grant waiver of university graduation requirements and credit for university work at the University of Utah in 1968. On the basis of data available at that time (percentile rankings of students finishing their sophomore year at a representative group of colleges and universities scattered over the United States plus very limited data on cutoff scores established by other colleges and universities), the Credits and Admissions Committee, in consultation with the General Education Council, established scores for waiver and for credit in the areas covered by the General Examinations. At the University of Utah Testing Center fewer than 200 students took the examinations from their inception in 1968 through December 1970. Nearly 800 took the examinations in the first seven months of 1971, and close to 1,300 in the months of August, September, and October of 1971. No objections to the testing program were raised in the first years of operation, when it affected a relatively small number of students, but when the number taking the examination increased so dramatically and the number of students obtaining credit appeared to be perhaps excessive, many questions were raised concerning the program. In particular, there appeared to be the feeling that there should have been an immediate review of the use of CLEP, with at least a cessation of all encouragement of still more students to attempt the examinations, when the number of students receiving credit first began to grow rapidly.

At an early meeting in Autumn Quarter 1971, the Credits and Admissions Committee discussed with Dean Franklin L. McKean the gathering of data that would permit an intelligent decision on modifications of the use of CLEP that might be required, including the possibility that such use should be totally discarded. On the basis of a preliminary study, the committee on November 10 recommended a moratorium on the awarding of CLEP credit and waiver of requirements until reconsideration of the program could be accomplished. Since the examinations program on this campus is part of a statewide program endorsed by the State Board of Higher Education, the committee recommended that the giving of the examinations at the University of Utah Testing Center be continued but that students be informed that after the month of November the university reserved the right to set new cutting scores and to change the amount of credit that might be offered.

On recommendation of its Executive Committee, the University Senate on December 6, 1971, adopted the following resolution:

> Moved that the principle of competency testing be strongly endorsed and supported, and further that the operation of the CLEP program, under present rules which allow for credit and waiver, be temporarily suspended after the January tests for the purpose of making a careful study and evaluation of the program, with a final decision as to the method of administration of competency testing to be reached within 90 days following the date of the January CLEP tests. Administration of the CLEP test, however, will continue during the period of credit suspension.

The Credits and Admissions Committee was asked to conduct a thorough review of the program with Dean McKean's office to assist in collection of data. Since the program had grown so explosively in size, and the type of students taking the examinations had changed from being well above average during the first two years to only slightly above average in the last group, there is no long-term data on how students who received credit on the basis of CLEP examination performed in their later years at the university. Any decisions reached at this time must be considered as subject to review, as further experience in the program is obtained. The report which follows is based on consultations by the committee with departments and groups most directly involved and on our analysis of the data presently available.

IMMEDIATE RECOMMENDATIONS

There was essentially unanimous agreement among those consulted with the principle that competency testing via examination with the waiver of graduation requirements and/or the granting of credit was appropriate and that the university should be engaged in seeking appropriate methods of determining the abilities of its students who have acquired knowledge outside regular courses of study. Under immediate consideration are the CLEP *General* Examinations, the set of five examination in English, humanities, mathematics, natural sciences, and social sciences–history which have been given on a routine basis at the University of Utah and elsewhere in the state since 1968. There also are CLEP examinations over specific *subject* areas. While several departments are interested in the *Subject* Examinations, there has been no extensive use of these examinations to date on this campus, and they are not considered in this section of this report.

Four of the General Examinations are divided into sections with scores reported separately as follows:

General Examination	Subareas
Humanities	Fine arts, literature
Mathematics	Skills, content
Natural sciences	Biological, physical
Social sciences–history	Social sciences, history

On the basis of its study of the examinations and their normalization and the limited reports obtained from departments, the committee, in 1968, decided that a student receiving a score of 450 or higher on a general examination or 45 or higher on a subscore corresponding to a specific university area would receive 12 hours credit in that area. The student receiving a score between 390 and 450 (or 39 and 45 for a subscore) would receive waiver of the university requirement in the area, but no credit. The significance of these scores in terms of percentile ranking is listed on the attached table. Twelve hours of credit were granted in each of the areas, English, social and behavioral sciences, physical sciences, mathematics, fine arts, and biological sciences, subject to a maximum total of 48 hours in accordance with university regulations limiting total credit by examination. In addition, waiver of the university requirement in American Institutions was granted on the basis of the score on the history subscore.

The committee in its current review first decided that any decisions on these examinations should be generally in accordance with the policies it has established as a basis for its consideration of petitions for transfer of credit from non-accredited institutions or credit for study off campus. These are as follows:

1. The work for which credit is given should be at a level comparable to work in this university.

2. The work need not necessarily correspond to any specific course given in this university, but should be in a general area in which the university has a program of study.

3. The group best suited to advise whether study at another university or off campus is of university caliber is the faculty of the department or departments most closely related to the area of study.

The findings of the committee are presented in four parts, three on specific areas, the fourth on the area of General Education.

Mathematics:

The university has no specific requirement in mathematics either for entrance or for graduation. The mathematics department states the CLEP General Examination in mathematics does not correspond to the work in any specific university course and is mostly over areas of mathematics which are below university level. On this basis the department of mathematics recommends that no credit be given for the CLEP General Examination in mathematics. The committee concurs with the recommendation.

American Institutions:

The requirement in American Institutions was instituted by the university in response to an act of the Utah State Legislature, Senate Bill 38, 1963, "an act requiring a reasonable understanding of the fundamentals of the history and principles and form of the government of the United States as a basis for responsible citizenship." The Faculty Council action of January 5, 1966, implies that the departments of economics, history, and political science are delegated the authority to decide when students have satisfied the legal requirement established by the legislature. The chairmen of those departments have reviewed the CLEP social sciences–history General Examination and report to us that in their opinion it is not sufficiently directed to the areas specified under the law. The committee believes their recommendation is controlling under the circumstances existing and recommends that no waiver of American Institutions requirement be granted on the basis of the CLEP General Examinations.

English:

The university requires the completion of two 2-hour courses in English composition for graduation. The department of English indicated they have serious reservations concerning the extent to which any multiple choice examination can adequately measure the ability of a student in English composition. However, they recognize that there will be some correlation between ability on the CLEP examination and in composition. After discussion both in the department of English and in the committees over conflicting proposals, the department recommended, as an interim measure while further information is gathered, the setting of the cutting score so that approximately 20 percent of entering freshmen are excused from, and receive credit for, English composition and that no waiver without credit be granted. Accepting this recommendation, the committee recommends that four credit hours in English composition be granted students receiving a score of 530 or higher on the CLEP General Examination in English.

General education:

The University Senate has established as a general requirement for graduation with a bachelor's degree the satisfaction of a general education requirement in four of the five areas: Western civilization, fine arts, social and behavioral sciences, life sciences, and physical sciences.

The University Senate delegated authority, subject as usual to its review, to the General Education Council operating under the dean of general education to list courses fulfilling the requirements in each area, to sponsor new courses, especially interdepartmental offerings, where it believed it advisable, and otherwise generally to administer the program of general education. There is no simple correspondence between departments and the areas of general education. The departments of history, speech, and philosophy each have courses accepted in three different areas. The department of geography has courses accepted in four different areas. Hence, the Credits and Admissions Committee felt that it should work primarily with the council on general education and generally be guided by its advice. However, the committee felt it also had a responsibility to the Faculty and University Senate to request directly the views of departments and to consider whether the evidence so received warranted a recommendation to the general education council to reconsider its decision or a report to the University Senate at variance with the views of the General Education Council.

It should be noted that the CLEP Subject Examination in Western civilization has been used to grant full credit or waiver in the American civilization area of general education. Only 36 persons have taken this examination at the University of Utah Testing Center during the period May 1969 through April 1972. The committee did not study the use of this (or any other) subject examination; neither was there mention of it in comments to the committee. Hence, the committee makes no recommendation at this time concerning change in the use of this examination.

Dean Oakley Gordon and the chairman of the committee each sent a request to all department chairmen and deans who might in any way be involved in general education requesting comment concerning the use of the CLEP General Examinations in the general education program. Each notice contained a tentative proposal. The committee proposal was to proceed as in the past except that the cutoff score for 12 hours credit in each area would be raised from 45 to 50. (As a matter of convenience, subscores on the CLEP General Examinations are presented on a 20-to-80 scale; scores on entire examinations on a 200-to-800 scale.) The tentative proposal by the General Education Council was as follows:

Score	Credit Granted	Requirements Satisfied
45	4	1 course in area
50	8	2 courses in area
55	12	Entire area requirement

After receiving comment from departments, the General Education Council gave its recommendation to the Credits and Admissions Committee. The council report stated that it had received comments varying from recommendations that the old cutoff scores of 39 for waiver and 45 for full credit be retained to statements that the examinations, or at least some of them, bore no relationship whatsoever to the kind of work given at the university and should not be used at all. The final recommendation of the council was that their proposal as first outlined seemed generally agreeable, was a reasonable compromise, and so was their final recommendation. It should be noted that the General Education Council also proposed that there should be continuing study of the adequacy of CLEP, including a study of alternatives, and that the dean of general education and the council indicated that they desired to work with departments in such studies. The Credits and Admissions Committee considered the recommendations in the light of the comments received by it. Again, these ranged from an endorsement of the initial, very generous standards to substitution of requirements that would grant credit to a negligible number of students or none at all. The committee decided that the general education proposal, that subscores of 45, 50, and 55 be accepted as satisfying one-third, two-thirds, or all of a general education requirement, with 4, 8, or 12 hours of credit granted, respectively, and no waiver without credit, was preferable to the modification it had initially proposed. Hence, the committee concurs with the recommendation of the General Education Council.

An additional problem should be noted here. The current *General Education Bulletin* (1971–1972) promotes CLEP testing by asking, "Is the thought enticing that you might suddenly find yourself a sophomore after a day of tests?" This promises more than CLEP testing can deliver in a number of cases. For example, prerequisite requirements for many courses are not satisfied by CLEP tests, nor is CLEP credit accepted toward departmental majors in the majority of cases.

RECOMMENDATIONS FOR ACTION

The Credits and Admissions Committee recommends that credit be granted on the basis of the College-Level Examination Program General Examinations as follows:

1. Mathematics: no credit.

2. American institutions requirement: no credit.

3. English: 4 credit hours in English composition for a score of 530 or better.

4. General Education: credit be granted in the area of social and behavioral sciences, life sciences, physical sciences, and fine arts on the basis of subscores on the examinations in social sciences, biological sciences, physical sciences, and fine arts, respectively.

Score	Credit Granted	Requirements Satisfied
45	4	1 course in area
50	8	2 courses in area
55	12	Entire area requirement

5. Total credit granted shall be subject to the existing 48-hour limitation on credit by examination.

6. There be no granting of waiver of a general university requirement without the simultaneous granting of credit for that requirement.

7. The General Education Bulletin should be revised and counseling should be modified so that a student will not be led to have undue expectations about the benefits of CLEP testing.

ADDITIONAL RECOMMENDATIONS

The department of English has indicated its desire to explore the possibility of administering a writing exercise to the students achieving credit in composition by CLEP. The comparison of writing ability with scores on the CLEP General Examination in English is essential in order to obtain information concerning the reliability of the test and the significance of the cutoff score. While there is an obvious budgetary problem connected with the grading of such writing exercises, the committee feels that it is important that such information be obtained and recommends that administrative consideration be given to the initiation of such a study.

Several departments indicated a desire to examine CLEP Subject Examinations for possible use in granting credit for specific courses. The committee believes it highly appropriate that nationally normalized examinations such as the CLEP Subject Examinations be used for the granting of credit and endorses such a study by departments. In such use there are two considerations which must be balanced.

1. The cutoff score for credit must be set sufficiently high to avoid compromise of the standards of the university.

2. The cutoff score should not be set at a level unreasonably high compared to the level of attainment of students in equivalent courses on campus.

It is recommended that any examination prepared on campus be tested on students enrolled in campus courses. It might be possible to utilize a CLEP examination in a campus class for normalization purposes. Dr. Pappas in the Counseling Center should be consulted.

In view of the developing pressures for credit by examination and credit for off-campus study, it is evident that the problems raised by CLEP will be with us for some time. The modifications of existing programs and installation of new ones to meet changing conditions should be effected in a climate of free and open discussion which will adequately consider traditional viewpoints, concern for liberal education, and the privileges and responsibilities of departments and colleges. Always, the relationship between symbols (hours of credit) and substance (what is learned— in the classroom, on the campus, by independent study) should be examined and evaluated.

Respectfully submitted,

Bruce F. Baird	Stephen W. Northam
Grant K. Borg	James P. Pappas
Arthur D. Broom	Sean M. Riley
R. Eliot Chamberlin	Orlando Rivera
Normand L. Gibbons	Frank J. Shaw
A. W. Grundmann	Irene M. Sturges
Frank B. Jex	Austin L. Wahrhaftig, Chm.

CLEP GENERAL EXAMINATIONS
Percentile Rankings of Three Populations* at Selected Scaled Scores

CLEP Scaled Score	English			Social Science†			Biological Science†			Physical Science†			Fine Arts†		
	I	II	III	I	II	III	I	II	III	I	II	III	I	II	III
600	83	94	97	83	90	93	85	87	96	83	80	94	83	92	No data available
550	70	85	91	69	75	83	69	74	88	73	66	84	71	74	
500	52	69	80	53	53	65	51	55	73	55	50	67	53	52	
450	32	47	63	32	31	44	32	33	52	38	29	46	34	30	
420	22	35	51	24	20	31	25	21	39	25	17	33	24	20	
390	15	22	39	16	11	21	17	14	27	13	8	22	15	11	

* Numerals I, II, III represent the following populations:

    I. Percentiles of national normalization sample: college and university sophomores at representative institutions.

    II. Percentiles for entering freshmen at University of Utah, autumn 1971, who took CLEP.

    III. Estimated percentiles for total entering freshman class at University of Utah, autumn 1971.

† Subtest norms.

How can colleges work together on transfer of credit?

Whose interests are at stake?

Cecil L. Patterson received a Ph.D. in English at the University of Pennsylvania. He is currently vice chancellor for academic affairs at North Carolina Central University and is actively involved with several organizations, including the Commission on Educational Credit Advisory Committee on Credit by Examination and Other Testing Programs, American Council on Education.

Interinstitutional Aspects of Credit by Examination in North Carolina

CECIL L. PATTERSON

The large number and the great variety of postsecondary education institutions in the state make transfer of credit a subject of intense interest in North Carolina. A 1979 count showed 115 postsecondary institutions, excluding a number of proprietary organizations, which offer work beyond high school. Forty-five of the 115 are senior institutions offering the baccalaureate or higher degree. The remaining 70 offer varying forms of associate degrees and other programs that lead to certificates requiring fewer than four years of attendance. Sixteen of the senior institutions are units of the state-supported University of North Carolina. Fifty-seven of the two-year institutions are parts of the publicly supported Department of Community Colleges. The balance of the institutions in both categories are privately supported. The institutions run the gamut from large, complex research institutions with five-figure enrollments to small units that offer a single associate degree for a student body numbering barely more than one hundred.

In addition to the traditional postsecondary institutions, a varying number of proprietary schools offer work beyond high school. These institutions are licensed by the Board of Governors of the University of North Carolina and, in some cases, also by agencies of the State Department of Public Instruction. Although these proprietary institutions are not included in the above count, they—and their students—claim that because they are licensed by the same agency responsible for the quality of the offerings of the traditional institutions, their credits should be accepted in transfer to any of the traditional schools. As a group, the postsecondary institutions offer curriculums ranging from the arts to agriculture to religion. They give and recognize credit obtained in a variety of ways ranging from "life experience" to credit by examination.

Because transfer among so many and so varied colleges is

complex and difficult, over the years the colleges have evolved a system to guide the transfer operations. They have attempted to institutionalize standards for transfer of credit so that a student can determine in advance what kind of credit will be accepted at what colleges, and so that an institution can determine before-hand whether credits from a program it plans to develop will be valid at other institutions in the state.

I have been asked to consider the interinstitutional aspects of credit by examination in North Carolina. The acceptance of credit by examination, however, is embedded in the overall system for accepting transfer credit. It seems more profitable, therefore, to consider the total North Carolina transfer system than to focus on the acceptance of credit by examination alone. The broader picture will give a clearer understanding and a more accurate description than will a limited analysis of just credit by examination.

The North Carolina transfer system is a formalized, informal system. By this I mean there is an organized structure, which is generally known but which no one is required to adopt, with a set of guidelines that nobody is compelled to follow. The operative agency of the system is the Joint Committee on College Transfer Students (JTC). The JTC is sponsored by the North Carolina Association of Colleges and Universities, and its membership derives from three cooperating agencies—the University of North Carolina, the North Carolina State Board of Education, and the Association of Independent Colleges and Universities. These four bodies represent all of higher education in North Carolina.

There are 12 official members of the JTC—4 appointed by each of the three cooperating agencies—and usually 5 ex officio members. One ex officio member is appointed by the North Carolina Association of Colleges and Universities and one by each of the three cooperating agencies. The immediate past chairman of the JTC becomes the fifth ex officio member. Some financial support is provided by the University of North Carolina, and the ex officio member appointed by the university serves also as the secretary and principal staff for the committee.

As adviser to the four participating agencies, the JTC is charged with smoothing the transfer of students from two-year institutions to senior colleges and universities. That work also affects lateral (intra-two-year and intra-four-year) transfers of students. The committee works mainly by developing consensus and then publishing that agreement for the information and guidance of all concerned.

Typically, the JTC operates through articulation subcommittees, which consist of members of the faculty, staff, and administration of the various colleges and universities. When a problem in transfer of credit comes to the attention of the JTC, the committee appoints an articulation subcommittee composed of members of the kinds of institutions affected by the problem. The number of committee members varies with the difficulty and the extent of the problem. The number may range from 5 to 50, but usually is from 6 to 10 members. Also, the chairman of the JTC and one or more official members are designated as resource and contact persons for the articulation subcommittee.

The articulation subcommittee confers with the people and the institutions experiencing the problem and attempts to develop a consensus on how to enable the student to transfer the credit with minimal loss and trouble. The results of these deliberations are reported by the articulation subcommittee, and a set of recommendations is submitted to the JTC. The committee considers the recommendations and, if necessary, solicits additional comments from the other institutions and recirculates the proposed recommendations among the institutions that are part of the problem. When these comments are returned, the JTC reaches a consensus, which it publishes as a recommendation for handling the problem.

These articulation subcommittees cover a wide range of problems regarding the transfer of credit. In 1977, 11 subcommittees dealt with the transfer of credit in such areas as criminal justice, nursing education, health education, and general education as well as the format of the transcript itself. The subcommittees conducted over 15 "articulation conferences" and involved in their work over 200 members of the faculty, staff, and administration of the various institutions.

The revision of the transfer guidelines for the area of general education illustrates both the kinds of problems the JTC handles and its approach to them. The problem first surfaced as an apparent difficulty in transferring credits for beginning English courses in the technical institutes. Typically, students from a technical institute present at least three English courses with descriptions like these:

ENGLISH

Course Title		Hours Per Week		Quarter
		Class	Lab	Hours Credit

T-Eng 101 Grammar   3   0   3
Designed to aid the student in the improvement of self-expression in grammar. The approach is functional with emphasis on grammar, diction, sentence structure, punctuation, and spelling. Intended to stimulate students in applying the basic principles of English grammar in their day-to-day situations in industry and social life.
Prerequisite: None

T-Eng 102 Composition   3   0   3
Designed to aid the student in the improvement of self-expression in business and technical composition. Emphasis is on the sentence, paragraph, and whole composition.
Prerequisite: T-Eng 101

T-Eng 103 Report Writing   3   0   3
The fundamentals of English are utilized as a background for the organization and techniques of modern report writing. Exercises in developing typical reports, using writing techniques and graphic devices, are completed by the students. Practical application in the preparation of a full-length report is required for each student at the end of the term. This report must be related to something in his or her chosen curriculum.
Prerequisite: T-Eng 102

The typical freshman English courses at the senior institutions, however, bear descriptions like these at North Carolina Central University:

110   English Composition (3 semester hours)
      A study of the essentials of composition and rhetoric. Emphasis on written work covering the several forms of composition.
120   English Composition (3 semester hours)
      Prerequisite: English 110
      A continuation of English 110.

At a regular meeting of the JTC, representatives of the technical institutes complained that their students were having difficulty getting English courses transferred for credit to the senior institutions. Senior institution members replied that they could not accurately tell what these descriptions meant and that they were uncertain whether the sequence of three courses was meant to equal the first two English courses in the four-year schools. Moreover, they pointed out that T-Eng 101 was called grammar and was therefore suspect as a remedial — thus unacceptable — course. Some senior institution representatives indicated that the designation T-Eng automatically made the whole sequence suspect.

The JTC decided to set up an articulation subcommittee to look into the problem. In choosing the members of the subcommittee, however, the JTC discovered that a large number of liberal arts courses in the technical institutes and the community colleges were suffering from this same kind of suspicion and lack of acceptance. They resolved, therefore, to expand the subcommittee and have it examine the whole question of the transferability of credits from courses normally included in the General Education Program (GEP).

The JTC named a widely respected GEP specialist, the vice chancellor for academic affairs of one of the University of North Carolina campuses, as chairman of the GEP subcommittee. Authorized to select a representative membership for the subcommittee, he selected 10 individuals, 3 of whom were from the JTC, and subdivided them into three study teams: humanities, sciences, and social sciences. The chairmen of these teams selected additional persons from the academic community. The total number eventually reached 17.

Each of these teams studied the policies, practices, purposes, and content of their particular area in the GEP. Team members studied the literature on the GEP and examined the philosophy and the organization of the programs, both throughout the nation and particularly in North Carolina. The teams held "miniarticulation conferences" in which they discussed various aspects of the GEP with faculty and administrators from a wide range of state institutions. Periodically the teams met with the GEP subcommittee as a whole and with the JTC to report progress.

After more than a year of such meetings, the GEP subcommittee had developed several alternative approaches to the problem. It could specify the competencies expected of the General Education Program, it could compile a list of recommended courses, or it could distill the essence of the various programs in the state and offer a common list of courses from those programs.

When the GEP subcommittee presented these alternatives to the JCT, it was decided to combine all of them into one approach. The JTC would recommend a model GEP representing the most commonly accepted categories of courses and, within those categories, describe the kinds of content that would most likely achieve the goals the majority of the General Education Programs attempted to reach. The JTC then adopted this approach as part of the revised guidelines for transfer for all GEP courses and published the recommendations as part of its regular publication program.

The Joint Committee on College Transfer Students distributes two major publications: *Guidelines for Transfer* and *Policies of Senior Colleges and Universities Concerning Transfer Students from Two-Year Colleges in North Carolina*. Normally updated every two years, the two publications appear in alternate years. The latest *Guidelines* was published in February 1977. The *Policies*, updated in 1976, was scheduled for revision in 1978 and was published in April 1979.

The *Guidelines* is a set of recommendations embodying the consensus developed by the JTC among the two-year and the senior institutions. The recommendations cover admissions,

General Education Program requirements, and transferability of credit—credit by atypical means, credit by examination, and credit for technical courses. Included are detailed suggestions for the number of hours of credit given for individual courses as well as model curriculums for various subject-matter fields and general education programs. A special section of the *Guidelines*, which concerns credit by examination, is presented at the end of this chapter in Appendix 1. A model GEP and descriptions of some "typical" courses are attached as Appendix 2.

In summary, acceptance of credit by examination is recommended for standardized tests such as those of the Advanced Placement Program, the National Achievement Examinations, and the CLEP Subject Examinations and General Examinations—and also for various institutional examinations.

The *Policies* is a compendium of the policies and procedures of the senior institutions regarding transfer students from two-year colleges. The publication lists the senior institutions individually and provides information on financial aid, fees, admissions, housing, maximum transferable hours accepted from two-year institutions, minimum hours the student must complete to earn the bachelor's degree, grade calculation procedures, and general education requirements, plus such detailed information as whether religion courses are accepted, whether nontraditional system credits are accepted, and whether (and how) credit is recognized for courses bypassed because of advanced placement. As a sample, the 1979 listing for North Carolina Central University is included as Appendix 3.

The *Policies* manual is intended for students and their advisers. By using it, students can match their present attainments with the schools that will accept most of their credits and provide the smoothest possible transition. The *Guidelines* is of major value to institutional administrators charged with developing curriculums in two-year institutions, evaluating transcripts in senior institutions, or developing policies for handling transfer students.

How well does the system work? There are two obvious gaps. The system is directed wholly inward. There is no mention of out-of-state students. Also, since compliance is voluntary, there are obviously some schools that do not follow the guidelines.

Other than not attending those schools, students have no recourse against this failure to comply. These schools, though, are a diminishing minority and are under a variety of overt and covert pressures to mend their ways. The guidelines represent agreements made among the members of the organizations representing all of higher education in North Carolina. These agreements, reached by the actions of the faculty and the staff members of the individual institutions, are published and widely disseminated so that they are available to every school and student.

Some figures will indicate the scale of the transfer operations as well as how effectively the system operates. In fall 1975, according to figures given in the *Statistical Abstract of Higher Education in North Carolina, 1975–1976,* 12,326 undergraduate transfer students enrolled in the colleges and universities of North Carolina. Of this number 4,132 transferred from two-year to senior institutions, 1,251 from senior to two-year institutions, 2,796 among senior institutions, 763 among two-year institutions, and 3,384 from out-of-state schools. This flow of transfers constituted 8.6 percent of the total undergraduate enrollment in the state. This amount is not only a significant percentage of the enrollment, but it also seems to indicate an acceleration of the trend toward transfers. The 12,326 transfers in 1975 represented a 10.9 percent increase over the number for 1974, which itself was an increase of 5.2 percent over 1973. Because similar statewide data are not yet available for 1976–77 and 1977–78, it is not yet possible to determine whether the trend is continuing.

On the specific question of transfer of credit obtained by examination, the *Policies* manual indicates that most institutions will accept such credit in transfer. The data for the manual are obtained through questionnaires completed by the senior institutions; the information is usually furnished by a dean or an admissions officer. The 1976 *Policies,* which includes responses from all 45 senior institutions, states that 27 (60 percent) accepted credit obtained through institutional or departmental examination; 36 (80 percent) accepted CLEP Subject credit; 37 (82.2 percent) accepted CLEP General credit; and 30 (66.6 percent) accepted credit for courses bypassed through advanced placement. Although these figures apply specifically to credit transferred from two-year to senior institutions, they are probably also valid for transfers among senior institutions. The questionnaire allows the senior institutions to indicate whether their policies differ for accepting transfer credit from two-year institutions and from senior institutions. Invariably the senior institutions reported that their policies were "essentially the same" for other senior institutions as for two-year colleges. There were no comparable data for intra-two-year transfers. The number (763) of such transfers, however, was relatively small; and any policy adopted by the two-year schools would have little effect on the overall status of the acceptance of credit by examination. Few senior institutions limit the amount of credit by examination they will accept from two-year schools. Where such a limit is set, it is usually 15 to 30 semester hours.

Moreover, once credit by examination has been accepted in transfer, in most senior institutions it becomes indistinguishable from other credits accepted in transfer. Twenty-five (55.5 percent) of the senior institutions indicated that they record on their transcripts only the courses and hours—not grades—for which the transfer credit is accepted. The remaining institutions follow various practices—from simply listing the total number of hours accepted to listing the courses, hours, and grades exactly as they are given on the transcript of the sending institution. To the extent that the practice of the majority of the senior institutions is adopted, credit by examination in North Carolina will enjoy the same status as credit transferred by any other means.

This acceptance indicates the strength and the potential of the North Carolina system for handling transfer credit. Despite the apparent concentration on in-state students, the out-of-state student is not necessarily penalized. Although the agreements are made among North Carolina colleges and universities, the categories agreed on are kinds of credit and types of institutions, not kinds of students. The distinctions among institutions are based on accreditation, not location. Instead of out-of-state and in-state students, the system "sees" just students—students who offer for transfer credit obtained by various means. The failure to refer to out-of-state students does not imply their exclusion. In 1975 out-of-state students constituted 27 percent of the total transfers, which indicates that the lack of mention did not effect their exclusion, either.

The apparent lack of recourse of the individual student against institutions that do not abide by the guidelines may not be so crippling as, at first glance, it may seem. The system is institutionalized and formalized rather than individualized and ad hoc. Organizations and agencies can carry on the battle for the student.

The North Carolina system has the other drawbacks typical of voluntary systems. It is slow, and it cannot order and force colleges to do anything. But the system does offer the benefits of freedom. It preserves the autonomy of the individual institutions. It provides a forum for the consideration of new problems as they arise. Its "guidelines" approach covers a wide range of transfer credit possibilities. By including the spectrum of possible ways of obtaining credit, the system shields such procedures as credit by examination and other atypical means from individualized attacks. The number and the variety of participating institutions mean that the system's potential is limited only by their ability to cooperate to achieve their goals. To the extent that the colleges can join their efforts to smooth the path of the student who transfers credit, the North Carolina voluntary, "institutionalized" approach to the problem of transfer credit may well be a viable alternative to a regimented, state-dictated system.

Appendix 1:
Transferability of Credit Obtained through Atypical Methods*

1. Credit by Examination
   a) Advanced Placement Program (APP) of the College Entrance Examination Board
      (1) Receiving institutions should consider acceptance of transfer

---

* From *Guidelines for Transfer: Recommendations of the Joint Committee on College Transfer Students.* Chapel Hill: University of North Carolina, General Administration, February 1977, pp. 8–9. Reprinted by permission of the publisher.

credits which have been awarded on the basis of APP scores of five (5) and four (4).

(2) Receiving institutions should consider acceptance of transfer credits which have been awarded on the basis of APP scores below four (4) when validated by follow-up courses within the same discipline.

b) National Achievement Examinations

When national achievement examination scores are too low to be consistent with the receiving institution's policies, transfer credit should be awarded if validated by follow-up courses in the same discipline taken at either the sending or receiving institution.

c) College-Level Examination Program (CLEP) of the College Entrance Examination Board

(1) The CLEP General Examinations

(a) All institutions of higher education are encouraged to make use of the CLEP General Examinations to the extent and in a manner appropriate to institutional purposes and curricular requirements.

(b) Institutions which adopt the General Examinations are encouraged to award credit for scores at or above the 25th percentile of the national sophomore norms of the General Examinations — the minimum recommendation of the College Entrance Examination Board.

(2) The CLEP Subject Examinations

(a) All institutions of higher education are encouraged to adopt the use of CLEP Subject Examinations to an extent appropriate to curricular requirements. Credits should be awarded for scores at or above the average score made by "C" students in the national norms for the Subject Examinations — the minimum recommendation of the College Entrance Examination Board.

(b) Receiving institutions should accept directly in transfer both *elective* and *required* credits awarded on the basis of CLEP Subject Examinations to the extent appropriate to curricular requirements.

(c) Receiving institutions should accept for transfer credits in the *major* field of study awarded on the basis of CLEP Subject Examinations.

d) Institutional Examinations

(1) Receiving institutions should accept directly in transfer both elective and required credits awarded on the basis of insti-

tutional examinations to the extent appropriate to curricular requirements.

(2) Receiving institutions should accept in transfer credits in the *major* field of study awarded on the basis of institutional examinations.

2. College-Level Courses Completed Prior to Graduation from the Secondary School

College-level courses completed at accredited collegiate institutions prior to secondary school graduation should be evaluated in the same manner as other courses which may appear on the institution's transcripts.

3. Military Service Credit

Each institution of higher education should be encouraged to use the American Council on Education (ACE) Examination, institutional examinations, or CLEP in determining credit to be awarded for work completed in military schools and for experience.

4. Credit Classified as "Technical"

Credit for courses which are components of technical curricula may be transferred to a college or university upon validation of applicable course work through the receiving institution's normal procedures.

5. College-Level Courses Offered Through University and College Extension Centers or Contractual Programs

Receiving institutions should accept credit for college-level courses offered by accredited institutions in university or college extension centers and in contract with technical institutes.

6. Acceptance of Transfer Credit from Co-op Programs, Field Experience, and Field Placement

a) Institutions of higher education offering credit through co-op programs, field experience, and field placement should publicize the constructs of each program and the rationale upon which the credit is given.

b) If the experience is utilized as an integral part of the overall instruction within a specific course, credit assigned to such courses should be transferred in the same manner as for courses taught by traditional methods.

Appendix 2:
Model General Education Program
and Course Descriptions*

GENERAL EDUCATION

Institutions of higher education in the United States have in common these goals: (1) to assemble and communicate to their students a comprehensive representation of the knowledge, values, skills, and arts developed by mankind; (2) to provide an environment in which scholars, professionals, and artists, with access to the working tools which they require, are permitted to contribute to the development of knowledge; and (3) from the combination of (1) and (2) to provide a climate of opinion for faculty and students in which a respect for the wisdom of the past is joined to a reverence for the open and exploring mind, which recognizes that the search for truth and beauty is constantly an unfinished adventure.

Institutions of higher education in North Carolina have generally shared the conclusion that it is desirable to require their students to become knowledgeable of man's intellectual and aesthetic heritage and of the contemporary impulses playing upon that heritage, to become accustomed to the use of the modes of inquiry through which knowledge is acquired and refined, and to become so deeply committed to the ideas and values associated with this heritage as to establish an ongoing lifetime involvement with it. The schedule of requirements set up to achieve these objectives is often referred to as the *general education program.*

The following is recommended as a generally accepted definition of the general education requirement:

1. The general education program should comprise at least a third (40 to 45 semester hours; 60 to 68 quarter hours) of the total work leading to the baccalaureate degree.

2. Students should be required to distribute their studies in such a way that they will be encouraged to learn and experience a comprehensive representation of human knowledge and the arts. It is the conclusion of the North Carolina Joint Committee on College Transfer Students that recognition of the general classification of knowledge in the humanities, the physical sciences and mathematics, and the social and behavioral sciences provides a satisfactory framework within which to identify and

---

* From *Guidelines for Transfer: Recommendations of the Joint Committee on College Transfer Students.* Chapel Hill: University of North Carolina, General Administration. February 1977, pp. 17–24. Reprinted by permission of the publisher.

prescribe the distribution requirements of a program in general education. In addition the committee believes that achievement of a basic competence in English composition is an essential ingredient of such a program. The following guidelines are recommended for each of the general field distribution areas:

	Minimum Course Work[1] Recommended	
	Sem. Hrs.	*Qtr. Hrs.*
English Composition	6	9
Humanities and Fine Arts	12	18
Courses must be selected from at least three of the following discipline areas: music, art, theater, foreign languages, literature, philosophy, religion, and speech.		
Mathematics	6	9
At least one course in "academic" mathematics (algebra, trigonometry, calculus, etc.); the other unit may be selected from among other quantitative subjects (symbolic logic, business mathematics, computer science, etc.).		
Natural Sciences	6	9
Courses including accompanying laboratory work selected from among the following disciplines: biology, physical and earth or space sciences.		
Social Sciences	12	18
Courses must be selected from among at least three of the following discipline areas: anthropology, economics, geography, history, political science, psychology, and sociology.		
Total	42	63

1. It is recommended that institutions be receptive to the transfer of credit obtained through atypical methods including credit by examination.

3. One legitimate function of a general education program is to assist the student in deciding on a major by making available to him a wide range of subject areas. For this reason and because general education courses many times are survey and introductory courses in a discipline, they are often justifiably concentrated in the first two years of study. This, however, may work against two of the important functions of general education, that of showing the inter-relatedness of knowledge and its contemporary validity and that of encouraging the student to a lifetime commitment to becoming generally educated.

It is recommended, therefore, that some general education courses be offered beyond the first two years of study, although it is recognized students should be advised of scheduling problems they may encounter if many of the general education credits are not earned in the first two years.

4. Knowledge is constantly in development. In part, this is because new information is acquired; in part, it is because society's perception of the relationship of existing knowledge to current concerns is constantly in flux. Institutions of higher education respond to these changes by developing new courses of instruction; sometimes cross-disciplinary studies provide the most favorable vehicles for responding to new knowledge and theories. Such innovative courses, often developed at the cutting edge of emerging ideas, may provide for students the most memorable and meaningful experience in a general education program. It is recommended that institutions of higher education strive to develop flexible measures for recognizing in the transfer process the general education content of experimental, cross-disciplinary courses taken at other institutions.

LIBERAL ARTS AND BASIC SCIENCES

English Composition

Freshman Year
Strong emphasis on English composition in written and oral forms, including such specific preparatory exercises as vocabulary building, spelling principles, reading for speed and comprehension, basic speech arts and English grammar (six semester hours or nine quarter hours).

Mathematics

Two courses (totaling six semester hours or nine quarter hours) should be selected as follows: at least one course in "academic" mathematics (e.g., algebra, trigonometry, and calculus) and the other unit selected from quantitative subjects (e.g., symbolic logic, business mathematics, and computer science).

Freshman and/or Sophomore Year

1. For nonscience majors whose curriculum does not require a sequence of two or more calculus courses: recommendation of six semester hours or nine quarter hours of fundamental mathematics for graduation with content at post-high school level presented in survey form and selected from fundamentals of algebra; sets, relations, and functions; the real number systems; finite mathematical systems (modulo arithmetic); logic; statistics and probability with simple application to the social sciences; analytic geometry of the plane; graphs of relations; other geometries; basic notions of elementary integral and differential calculus.

2. For nonscience majors whose curriculum does not require a sequence of two or more calculus courses but who are better qualified students and/or whose future courses require a stronger background: same recommendation as item 1 above with a more rigorous treatment of listed topics.

3. For students whose curriculum (science, engineering, mathematics) requires a sequence of two or more calculus courses: recommendation of an offering which follows the Mathematical Association of America's *Commentary on a General Curriculum in Mathematics for College* (1972), page 6 (See Guideline 3 below).

a) Calculus with analytic geometry (nine semester hours or equivalent quarter hours).

b) Linear algebra (three semester hours or equivalent quarter hours).

Other Guidelines

1. The topics in item 1 above are to be covered at a level sufficient to prepare the student to take either:

a) A moderately rigorous calculus course.

b) A moderately rigorous course in modern algebra or linear algebra.

c) A moderately rigorous course in modern geometry.

2. For science and mathematics majors it is desirable that the minimum high school prerequisite for the course content be two years of algebra, one year of geometry, and one-half year of trigonometry.

3. Mathematics 1, *Introductory Calculus* (three semester hours or equivalent quarter hours) — differential and integral calculus of the elementary functions with associated analytic geometry.

Mathematics 2, 4, *Mathematical Analysis* (three semester hours or equivalent quarter hours each) — techniques of one-variable calculus, limits, series, multivariable calculus, differential equations.

Mathematics 3, *Linear Algebra* (three semester hours or equivalent quarter hours)—systems of linear equations, vector spaces, linear dependence, bases, dimensions, linear mappings, matrices, determinants, quadratic forms, orthogonal reduction to diagonal form eigenvalues, geometric applications.

Humanities and Fine Arts

Courses (totaling twelve semester hours or eighteen quarter hours) must be selected from at least three of the following discipline areas: art, drama, foreign languages, literature, music, philosophy, religion, and speech.

Freshman and/or Sophomore Year

The basic requirements of the humanities guidelines may be fulfilled through one of the following alternates:

1. An integrated humanities course (twelve semester hours or eighteen quarter hours) organized chronologically or by themes to show man's appreciative and creative roles in art, drama, literature, music, philosophy, and religion and taught by faculty members whose individual or collective breadth (e.g., team teaching) is sufficient in the above areas. Such an integrated humanities course may need to be broken down, for recording purposes, into more traditional titles in order to facilitate communication in transfer.

2. A block or sequence of courses (twelve semester hours or eighteen quarter hours) in at least four of the following areas:

    a) Art
    b) Drama
    c) Foreign Languages
    d) Literature
    e) Music
    f) Philosophy
    g) Religion
    h) Speech

Other Guidelines

1. Sequences should be determined by faculty advisors and guidance counselors in light of the student's educational goals.

2. Applied courses in art and music may not be used in meeting requirements of general education guidelines.

Art

Freshman and/or Sophomore Year

1. Senior institutions should accept for transfer credit courses which include:

a) Art appreciation
b) Drawing
c) Painting
d) Ceramics
e) Sculpture
f) Design
g) Art history survey

2. Two-year institutions should require a balanced program of general studies and art courses. The art courses should be varied and provide experiences with both two-dimensional and three-dimensional art work. Sequences of courses should be determined by art faculty advisors and counselors in light of the student's educational goals.

3. Students desiring to transfer into a Bachelor of Fine Arts or professional degree after the sophomore year may have to spend an additional semester or year in order to complete the program. Although it may be possible to complete the credit hour requirement during a two-year program, independent studio work, sequential courses, and the maturation of the student within a studio-oriented program may require more time.

Drama

Freshman and/or Sophomore Year

1. Institutions should accept for transfer credit courses which include:

a) Beginning acting
b) Introduction to theatre
c) Play production in activities courses
d) Scene and lighting design
e) Voice and diction
f) Stage crafts

2. Sequence of courses should be determined by faculty advisors and counselors in light of the student's educational goals.

3. Students desiring to transfer into a Bachelor of Fine Arts or professional degree program should be advised to transfer after one year to eliminate problems of transferability, mainly pertaining to participation and required degree courses.

Other Guidelines

1. Two-year colleges should provide an opportunity for students to explore the theatre, prepare in techniques and skills and develop cognate courses.

2. Students should take some cognate courses which may include:

a) Art appreciation, introduction to drawing and painting, design or drafting (if interested in design).

b) Music appreciation, beginning ballet or modern dance (if interested in acting and directing).

Foreign Language

Freshman Year

Emphasis on audio-lingual skills. The work is to be accepted at face value and credited toward total hours for graduation, with the understanding that these hours may be checked by a proficiency test or other means.

Sophomore Year

Stress on skills in reading and writing. In some cases, literary criticism may have a legitimate place.

Other Guidelines

1. A college should accept a high school student on the basis of preparation in the four language skills as recommended by foreign language programs of the Modern Languages Association. Literature receives no special emphasis in high school except for students seeking advanced placement.

2. Basically, high schools should concentrate on communications skills and colleges and universities on literature, advanced composition and syntax, and where possible, phonetics and applied linguistics (civilization where needed).

3. The idea of placement by years or units should be abandoned. For determination of performance in the skills, measurement should be by modern proficiency tests, whether administered by the junior or by the senior college at entrance. In respect to the different goals, resulting from institutional autonomy, some variation in the pattern may be necessary.

Literature

Freshman and/or Sophomore Year

Concentration upon an introduction to the study of masterpieces of literature.

Music

Freshman and/or Sophomore Year

1. Institutions should accept for transfer credit courses which include:

a) Music history

b) Music literature

c) Music appreciation

2. Students should receive credit in music history — literature without further examination, even from institutions which combine instruction in music literature and theory.

3. In recognition of the individual nature of instruction in applied music and the wide discrepancies in approach to instruction in music theory, diagnostic or placement examinations may be required in these areas. Audition and/or examination should be given as early as practical, certainly no later than admission to the senior institution.

Students should be advised of the results of placement examinations in music theory and should be allowed to make their own decisions regarding the repetition of previous courses. In the case of applied music, the placement results should be accepted as a specific guide to proficiency standing.

Other Guidelines

1. Four-year colleges should recommend alternatives to assist students for whom the sequence of information offers a dramatic change.

2. Two-year institutions are advised to examine the practices of the four-year departments and should avoid teaching those courses which are considered upper division.

Philosophy

Freshman and/or Sophomore Years

Study of philosophical issues relating to methods of reflective inquiry.

Appendix 3:
Sample Listing of Policies toward
Transfer Students*

North Carolina Central University
Durham, North Carolina   27707

ADMISSIONS

1.   Interested in two-year college student? *yes* Limit? *no*

2.   Require standardized tests for transfers? *yes*
     If so, which? *SAT if associate degree is not earned.*

* From *Policies of Senior Colleges and Universities Concerning Transfer Students from Two-Year Colleges in North Carolina, 1979–1980.* Chapel Hill: University of North Carolina, General Administration, 1979, pp. 49–50. Reprinted by permission of the publisher.

3. Minimum score required on #2 above? *yes*

4. Standardized tests required with one year of college work? *yes* associate degree? *no*

5. Require high school transcript for transfers? *With an associate degree - no.*

6. Must transfer student meet high school unit requirement? *Yes, without associate degree. 4 units-Eng.; 2-for. lang.; 1-soc. sci.; 2-math; 1-sci.; 6-electives.*

7. Campus interview is *optional.*

8. Associate degree is *required.*

9. Associate degree and recommendation improve chance of admission? *yes*

10. Is the associate of applied science degree from technical institute acceptable for junior status? *yes*

11. Is the associate of applied science degree from proprietary business college acceptable for junior status? *Yes, from one or two North Carolina schools.*

12. Minimum hours required before consideration? *No, only graduation.*

13. Accept out-of-state students? *yes*

HOUSING

14. On-campus housing available? *yes*

15. Mandatory for single students to reside in campus housing? *Yes* Men ( ) Women ( ) *unless 21 years of age, veterans or living at home.*

16. Housing for married students? *no*

COSTS

17. Fees for year 1978-79?

	In-State Students	Out-of-State
Tuition	$ 310.00	$ 2048.00
Required fees	262.00	262.00
Room	615.00	615.00
Board	640.00	640.00
Other *(laundry)*	31.00	31.00
Total	$ 1858.00	$ 3596.00

FINANCIAL AID

18. Available financial aid? *Acad., B.E.O.G., N.D.S.L., Loans, Work-Study, Athletic*

OTHER

19. Maximum transferable hours from a two-year college?
                                            (*60*) semester hours
                                            ( ) quarter hours
                        from a four-year college?
       Unlimited, but student must meet   ( ) semester hours
       residency requirements   ( ) quarter hours

20. Hours required for junior classification? *56 sem. hours*

21. Minimum hours student must complete at senior institution to
     earn degree? *64 sem. hours*

22. Are all courses attempted used in calculating cumulative
     average for admission? *yes*   Exceptions?

23. If course is repeated, only higher mark (*x*) both marks is/are
     used in calculating average ( ).

24. Include quality points from two-year college in computing
     cumulative average for graduation? *no*
     Admission to honor society? *no*

25. Assuming that student has "C" average on all work attempted at
     two-year college, courses on which the student earned a grade
     of "D": *will not transfer and student must retake any required*
     courses on which he earned this grade.

26. Grades from two-year colleges are recorded on senior college
     transcript: *listing only courses and credit hours transferred.*

27. Religion courses transfer? *yes*

28. Transfer of credit by (*x*) department exam (*x*) CLEP (*x*) USAFI?

29. Credit for bypassed courses as a result of advanced
     placement? *no*

30. Limit on transfer of credit by nontraditional means? *no*
     If yes, specifics:

31. From nontraditional system, we *seek data to allow equating*
     credit to our own system.

32. Credit from nonaccredited institutions? *no* If so, is there a
     difference if accredited sending institution has accepted the
     credit? *Yes, students may challenge courses in question by*
     taking an examination.

33. Credit granted from technical institute for: *general education*
     courses and some specialized courses.

34. Does credit granted from technical institute include general
     education courses? *yes*

35. Are individual courses from technical institute transferable? *yes* Any restrictions? *Must be part of associate deg. program.*

36. Are individual courses from proprietary business college transferable? *yes* Any restrictions? *Must be part of the associate degree program.*

37. Transfer policies regarding four-year institutions are: *essentially the same as for students from two-year institutions.*

38. Option concerning catalog degree requirements? *no*

39. Credit for interdisciplinary honors courses?

40. General education requirements: *(semester calendar)*

    English - *Communication skills (written and oral) - 3 courses*

    Foreign language - *See humanities and fine arts*

    Mathematics - *Four courses, not more than 2 in any one science, at least one must furnish lab. experience: biology,*
    Science - *information science, chemistry, math, psychology, geography, and physics*
    Social science:- *Three courses chosen from at least 2 depts: economics, geography, political sci., sociology, history, and psychology*
    Physical education - *and health education: 3 courses (3-9 hrs.) with not more than 2 courses to be taken in the same department*
    Other - *Humanities and fine arts - 6 courses to be chosen from at least 3 depts.: art, for. lang., (lang., lit. and/or linguistics), dramatic art, philosophy, English (lit. and/or linguistics), music*

Who stands to gain or lose?

How basic are the economic considerations?

Douglas M. Windham is a professor in the School of Education of the State University of New York at Albany. For the last two years he has served as director of the Comparative Education Center and codirector of the Educational Finance and Productivity Center of the University of Chicago. He received a Ph.D. in economics from Florida State University in 1969. He has written extensively for various publications. Professional activities include serving as a consultant, notably to the College Board CSS Committee on Need Assessment Procedures and to the Board on the economics of credit by examination. He is currently working on a study of individual accountability and individual choice in educational planning and also on a study of tuition economics in private higher education.

Economics of Credit Exemption

DOUGLAS M. WINDHAM

The interest of academic scholars and education administrators in the various systems that have evolved in the last two decades to evaluate prior learning experiences of college and university students has recently changed from polite regard to sharp concern. The issues of concern can be described as intellectually "high" and "low" roads.

The high road considers the ability of any examination or other evaluative instrument to substitute for classroom learning experiences; the danger that such degrees — totally or predominantly granted by examination or exemption — devalue the meaning of the baccalaureate and allow for potentially fraudulent actions against students; the potential abuse of such systems if they are used as a competitive device among institutions to attract students; and the controversy concerning the equity of a system that — while not explicitly biased by social class — tends to be perceived by many as a program predominantly for the economically advantaged.

The low road considers the financial self-interests of academics and administrators. I would not imply that these concerns are not legitimate matters for educators to ponder; the term "low" connotes only that it is not the educational effect on students that receives primary emphasis here but rather the institution's or the academic's self-interests. With or without the pejorative adjective, the divergent motivations of participants in the present reexamination of prior learning credits must be recognized. This is especially important because a significant portion of the current interest — expressed by educators in terms of objective educational issues — may have its source in primarily self-interested financial considerations. The concomitance of the recent higher education recession from 1970 to 1979 and the sudden widespread questioning of a program that heretofore was accepted, if not actually strongly endorsed, by most participants is the basis for the cynicism expressed in this paper.

Before proceeding, it would be useful here to distinguish among the major forms of recognized previous learning. Long before national systems of evaluation were instituted, many colleges and universities had already established programs allowing exemption—with or without credit—from distributional requirements or from graduation requirements. In the early 1950s the College Entrance Examination Board, with the assistance of the Fund for the Advancement of Education and the Carnegie Corporation, created the Advanced Placement Program (APP), which allowed students in high school to take courses that would, following the students' successful completion of examinations, eventually count toward college graduation. In 1966 the College-Level Examination Program (CLEP) was created to allow for a more general evaluation of previous learning experiences as a basis for granting postsecondary education credits. The CLEP program has expanded rapidly; in 1977–78 it involved more than 145,000 candidates, who registered for approximately 359,000 examinations. In comparison, in 1977–78 the Advanced Placement Program involved 93,300 students and more than 122,500 examinations, with 4,300 high schools participating in the program. No national data are available on individual institutional programs.

These figures indicate that the concern that these programs may reduce the effective demand for higher education is well founded. Before proceeding to a discussion of the possible effects of the widespread adoption of APP and CLEP, one additional system of credit recognition should be mentioned: the early admission plan whereby an institution of higher education allows a student to enter as a freshman after completing the eleventh grade. The student then pursues a normal college program. Early admission is a potentially important alternative to other forms of credit exemption because, in contrast to APP and CLEP, the college or university suffers no loss of revenue or demand for its instructional and related services. The fact that early admission programs allow the recognition of prior learning experiences while shifting costs to the secondary schools (which lose full-time equivalents because of fewer twelfth-grade students) has already made them controversial. If early admission is expanded to offset the potential effects of APP and CLEP activities, a serious conflict will arise between the interests of secondary school systems and those of postsecondary institutions.

At present there is no data base that would allow an evaluation of the amount and incidence of the costs and benefits associated with APP, CLEP, and early admission programs. Studies by Meyer (1975), Jamison and Wolfe (1976), McCluskey and Richmond (1975), and Kimmel (1976) have raised issues and posited models for such an analysis. The recent work commissioned by the College Board (*The Economic Impact of Credit by Examination Policies and Practices,* John R. Valley, editor, Educational Testing Service, 1978) has advanced this effort by presenting alternative research designs to evaluate the financial impact of prior-learning recognition.

In this paper I attempt to present a synthesis of excerpts of the literature cited above while incorporating my own perception of the appropriate emphasis that should be given to the selections. The concern here is with the effects of the programs. No attempt is made to evaluate the legitimacy of the recognition of prior learning as a basis for placement or credit; no attempt is made to evaluate the procedures or the instruments used in such programs. This does not imply a failure to recognize the importance or even the primacy of such issues; it is a recognition that this paper is only one of a set of papers dealing with the controversy over credit by examination and related devices and that colleagues whose training is more suitable for the evaluation of these other questions are already at work.

Ideally a credit exemption program evaluation would differentiate the costs and benefits among students, institutions, and society. It would also be appropriate to show whether certain subgroups of students, institutions, or both receive an unusual portion of the benefits or bear an unusual portion of the costs. Societal concerns deal mainly with the effect of credit exemption programs on support through taxation for higher education and on redistribution of user and nonuser inequalities.

Any evaluation of credit exemption must begin with answers to the following questions:

1. Who is eligible for credit exemption and who successfully takes advantage of it?

2. In what manner is the exemption granted?

3. Is credit exemption used for course requirements and distributional credit but not for graduation?

4. Is credit exemption used for reducing the total course load for graduation and, if so, does this reduction affect tuition payments by the student?

The answer to the first question is necessary if we are to examine the assertion (O'Hearne 1972) that the credit exemption program has a primary effect as a cost-reducing "scholarship" for academically able students. Given the correlation in United States society between ethnicity or race and certain academic disadvantages, this effect could be seen as a source of controversy. For example, if white students are shown to receive a disproportionate share of exemption credits, through whichever program, the effect could be to inflate the rate of return to higher education for that group (to the extent that exemptions reduce time and instructional fees). Defenders of credit exemption are then faced with the uneasy task of weighing the individual gains of some students against the offsetting costs in terms of the achievement of societal goals for greater ethnic and racial equality in access to higher education. The solution of such a conflict, of course, is not necessarily to restrict credit exemption. As in most problems of equality in higher education, the source and the solution lie in the home and the education system encountered earlier by the student.

The second question is necessary because different institutions provide credit exemption in different forms. If credit exemption is used only to allow the student to bypass certain introductory courses but does not affect distributional or graduation requirements, the effect on total institutional demand as well as on the demand for individual department instructional personnel will be minor. In contrast, if credit exemption affects distributional requirements, there is a potential for a redirection of demand for instruction, away from those departments whose courses are exempted and toward other departments. This redirection is in addition to the obvious effect of credit exemption's reducing the demand for faculty who offer introductory courses. The latter has a potentially serious effect on the demand for teaching assistants and thereby on the ease with which graduate students can finance their education.

Finally, if credit exemption can be used toward graduation requirements, the demand for course offerings in general could be decreased. If students are able to reduce the total number of quarters or semesters for which they have to register, they will pay less tuition, and the credit exemption programs will have reduced the institutional revenues. Concomitantly, there is the potential for an aggregate decline in the demand for instructional and support services.

This analysis is only a partial evaluation of possible results. The prediction of effects is complicated by a variety of factors. For example, students who receive credit exemption toward graduation may enroll in the same number of college terms but may take fewer courses in certain quarters or semesters. The effect on tuition depends on the structure of tuition charges. Most institutions in the United States charge full tuition for some minimum number of undergraduate course hours — for example, 12 course hours per quarter or semester. Full-time students often take 15 or even 18 course hours in a term without increasing the required tuition. Because of this tuition structure, a student may reduce the hours taken because of credit exemption but not affect the tuition paid to the institution.

Some students may use credit exemption to expand their programs and voluntarily take courses that, without the exemption program, they would not have had time for. In both examples tuition payments are the same as they would be without credit exemption, but in the first instance the demand for instructional services is reduced.

The situation is further complicated when part-time students are considered. For them, a rapidly increasing proportion of the higher education market, tuition is usually more closely linked to the actual number of courses taken in a particular term. Because of this and the unlikelihood that part-time students would be willing to take more courses than are required for graduation, credit exemption programs are likely to reduce tuition receipts and the demand for instructional and support services for this clientele.

As in the analysis of most demand situations, there is the possibility that any reduction in demand as a result of a credit exemption program may be offset by an increase in demand for institutional services by new students who are attracted to higher education (or to a particular institution) because of credit exemption availability. There is reason to doubt that credit exemption has increased the aggregate demand for education significantly enough to offset the probable tuition losses. The paucity of data and research in this area, however, means that little is actually known about the scale or the incidence of these effects.

While the foregoing has emphasized the institutional impact of credit exemption, the effect on students is also apparent. With one important exception the programs would appear to benefit students, who may reduce their tuition payments, save time, or both. The students may eliminate required redundancies in their academic programs and enroll in more enrichment courses; they may, at the very least, be able to structure their academic programs to accommodate their own perception of their abilities and needs.

The possible exception to this sanguine expectation is that credit exemption may dilute the quality of education received. If learning rather than graduating is the primary determinant for life success, and if credit exemption does reduce learning by precluding classroom experiences, then credit exemption could be a potential cost to students. This diluting effect remains open to sharp questioning, however, and in situations in which credit exemption leads to enriched rather than shortened college careers, the question is possibly irrelevant.

Table 1 presents a summary of the potential effects of different forms of credit exemption on institutions and students. Seven alternative higher education programs for granting credit for earlier achievement are listed in the first column: three uses of the AP Program, three uses of the CLEP-type credit-by-examination programs, and the early admission programs. As column two indicates, secondary schools are largely unaffected in terms of costs or benefits (if these effects are restricted to the impact on the full-time-equivalent funding base used in most states) except when colleges and universities allow eleventh-grade graduates to enroll as first-year higher education students. The present small scale of early admission programs should not lead one to discount too easily the potential impact if higher education institutions should expand early admission as a means of alleviating some of the potential "costs" of AP and CLEP programs. The AP Program may have a higher unit cost for secondary schools than the traditional curriculum has, but there is no evidence that the difference is substantial. The existence of AP and CLEP programs may increase student retention and levels of motivation, and these should be recognized as possible positive effects for secondary schools. The possibility of early admission could increase student motivation but would not have a strong enough effect on high school retention rates to offset the negative effect on the school of losing students for their full senior year.

Table 1 shows the reasons for the substantial concern about APP and CLEP in higher education. Although the use of credit exemption tests for placement or to alter distributional requirements may cause internal reallocations of demand for instructional services, the serious fiscal threat is in the reduction of the number of tuition-bearing courses required for graduation. As explained earlier, to the extent that this reduces tuition receipts, the university or the college finances the shortening of the student's program. The institutional incentive to emphasize increased use of early admission is obvious: The costs are shifted to the secondary school system.

The impact on students has been divided into three parts: the time required for graduation, the direct costs of education, and the quality of education received. The patterns indicate a strong positive influence in all three dimensions. Time is either reduced or unaffected; costs are either reduced or unaffected; and quality appears positive. The uncertainty about quality stems from uncertainty concerning the testing programs' ability to assure that successful students are prepared for the higher-level courses for which they become eligible. Although it seems fair to say that

Table 1

Incidence of Effects of Credit Exemption Programs

Credit Exemption Program	On Secondary Schools (FTE's demand for instructional services)	On Higher Education Institutions		On Individual Students		
		Tuition receipts	Demand for instructional services	Time savings	Direct cost savings	Quality of education
Advanced Placement Program						
Placement only	0	0	*	0	0	+?
For distributional exemption only	0	0	*	0	0	+?
For credit toward graduation	0	-?	-?	+	+?	+?
College-Level Examination Program						
Placement only	0	0	*	0	0	+?
For distributional exemption only	0	0	*	0	0	+?
For credit toward graduation	0	-?	-?	+	+?	+?
Early Admission Programs	—	0	0	+	+?	+?

NOTE: Zero (0) indicates that no benefit or loss occurs.
Plus (+) represents a probable benefit.
Questionable plus (+?) is a likely but uncertain benefit.
Minus (−) represents a probable loss.
Questionable minus (−?) is a likely but uncertain loss.
Asterisk (*) represents internal redistribution among levels and departments.

early admission programs, because of their greater selectivity, have less potential for problems, studies have indicated that academic success has not always been concomitant to an easy adjustment to the other dimensions of college life.

All the effects noted in Table 1 are only expectations deduced from assumptions about student and institutional reactions to these various programs. No data base now exists to allow the incidence of positive or negative effects on schools, colleges, and students to be calculated. The extensive use in this paper of modifying adjectives such as possible, probable, and potential is not an attempt to avoid decision but simply a recognition of reality. Before public and institutional debate on these programs can advance, it is necessary to develop a model that will allow both the individual institution and the social science researcher to estimate with confidence the direction and the scale of the effects of credit exemption programs.

The College Board is preparing a research program to examine two aspects of the credit exemption program. The first proposed study will involve a random sample of 5,000 students who have used the AP or CLEP programs, with stratification based on the number of examinations attempted. Five areas of information will be covered: test results, personal characteristics, high school experience, financial situation, and future plans. The desired outcome of this project is a better understanding of whether credit exemption programs lead to decreased time in college and to financial savings.

The second study will emphasize institutional concerns. A sample of institutions will be invited to cooperate in an assessment of the financial impact of credit-by-examination activities. The effect of full-time-equivalent levels and the relative size of course demand by departments, divisions, and levels (basic versus upper) will be analyzed. The primary purpose of this research is to produce a management model that can be used to evaluate the levels and the incidence of costs and benefits related to the institutional recognition of prior student learning (with an emphasis on APP and CLEP). The model should allow for the evaluation of the demand for faculty and the effects of credit recognition on the fixed, variable, and marginal costs of instructional services.

The effects of credit recognition on student as well as institutional finances will be considered as part of a general reexamination of the rationale for state, institutional, and personal financing of credit exemption programs.

[The College Board reports that this study began in November 1979 and that the initial phase will be completed in May 1980. The products of the phase one activities will include a listing of policy issues relating to the economic implications of recognizing prior learning through a variety of processes and the kinds of data a college needs to make decisions about alternative credit-by-examination policies.]

The potential importance of the College Board project, which is still in a formative stage, is not reduced by emphasizing the following: The financial considerations implicit in the economic analysis of credit exemption must always remain secondary to the more directly academic issues. The finding that credit exemption programs are costly for institutions in terms of lost tuition revenue should not be of great concern if the higher education community retains its confidence in the legitimacy of the credit exemption approach. Although the work of economists, accountants, and administrators on the economics of credit exemption will not provide automatic answers, it will provide information for the credit exemption debate. The answers can come only from the members of the academic community.

The greatest danger revealed by this paper's introduction to the economic issues in the debate is that financially the education community may face a "zero-sum" game. The benefits of credit exemption to the student may be purchased only at a cost to the education institution involved. In another zero-sum situation, higher education institutions may be tempted to expand early admission programs beyond justifiable limits simply to avoid the tuition losses resulting from other credit exemption programs. Finally, certain marginal institutions may become involved in the use of credit exemption as a competitive device against other, more responsible institutions. As in Gresham's law of monetary value—bad money drives out good—so, in an employment system increasingly dominated by credentialism, bad credits may drive out the good.

All these issues point out the crucial responsibility borne by the participants in the credit exemption debate. The economics of the matter is overwhelmingly important, but the answers will not come from economists alone, or even primarily. Credit exemption questions are subordinate to the resolution of the more basic issue of the purpose of postsecondary education. The difficulty in resolving the present quandary is a product of the inability to define that purpose.

BIBLIOGRAPHY

Abraham, A. *Time-Shortened Degree Mechanisms in Florida.* Florida Agricultural and Mechanical University, October 1977.

Apstein, B. "Dangers of Credit by Examination." *The Educational Forum*, Vol. 39, No. 3, March 1975, pp. 354–358.

Arbolino, Jack N. "... No Matter Where You Learned It." *The College Board Review*, No. 99, Spring 1976, pp. 13–20.

Archer, J. A., and H. C. Nickens. *Credit by CLEP: A Disconcerting Look at a Good Idea.* Virginia Western Community College, June 1975.

Bersi, Robert M., and Mary Ann Harp. "Restructuring the Baccalaureate: A Focus on Time-Shortened Degree Programs in the United States." Washington, D.C.: American Association of State Colleges and Universities, 1973.

Boulding, Kenneth E. "The Management of Decline." *Change*, 7, June 1975, pp. 8ff.

Bowen, Howard R. "Time, Informal Learning, and Efficiency in Higher Education." *Education Record*, 54, Fall 1973, pp. 271–280.

Boyer, Ernst L. "Shorter Time for Undergraduate Degrees," in Winfred Godwin and Peter D. Mann, eds., *Higher Education: Myths, Realities and Possibilities.* Atlanta: Southern Regional Educational Board, 1972.

Caldwell, E. "Analysis of an Innovation (CLEP)." *The Journal of Higher Education*, Vol. 44, No. 9, December 1973, pp. 698–702.

Caldwell, E. "In-College Effects of Acceleration by Examination." *Journal of College Student Personnel*, September 1977, pp. 399–402.

Carnegie Commission on Higher Education. *Less Time, More Options: Education beyond High School.* New York: McGraw-Hill, 1971.

Casserley, P. L. *College-Level Examination Program: Its Meaning to Participants.* College Entrance Examination Board Research and Development Reports, Educational Testing Service, April 1973.

Committee for Economic Development. *The Management and Financing of College.* New York: 1973.

Crary, Lowell L., and Larry L. Leslie. "The Private Costs of Postsecondary Education." Tucson: University of Arizona, 1977. Mimeographed.

Cross, K. Patricia, John R. Valley, et al. *Planning Non-Traditional Programs: An Analysis of Issues for Postsecondary Education.* San Francisco: Jossey-Bass, 1974.

Dresch, Stephen P. "A Critique of Planning Models for Postsecondary Education." *Journal of Higher Education,* Vol. 46, May–June 1975a, pp. 245–286.

Dresch, Stephen P. "Impact of Student Aid and Labor Market Conditions on Access to Postsecondary Education: Technical Proposal." New Haven: Institute for Demographic and Economic Studies, June 1975b. Mimeographed.

Froomkin, Joseph. *Recent Developments in Postsecondary Education.* Washington, D.C.: Joseph Froomkin, Inc., January 1976.

Fund for the Advancement of Education. "They Went to College Early." Evaluation Report No. 2. New York: 1957.

Furlong, T. E. "The Perceptions of Selected Groups of University and Community College Administrators of the College-Level Examination Program and Its Implications for the State Universities and Community Colleges of Florida." Dissertation, Florida State University, August 1977.

Hadley, E. E. *Credit–No Credit Course Options and Credit by Examination as Policy Variables Affecting Freshman Performance.* Drake University, June 1974.

Hanson, E. O. "An Investigation of the Validity of the College-Level Examination Program's General Examinations and a Review of Related Issues in Higher Education." Dissertation, Weber State College, September 1973.

Hoenack, Stephen A. "Direct and Incentive Planning within a University." *Socio-Economic Planning Sciences,* Vol. 11, 1977b.

Jamison, D. T., and B. B. Wolfe. "Assessment and Accreditation Economic Considerations," in W. Willingham and E. Nesbitt, eds., *Implementing a Program for Assessing Experiential Learning.* Princeton, N.J.: CAEL, Educational Testing Service, 1976.

Jamison, D. T., and B. B. Wolfe. "The Economics of Experiential Learning Programs." *Findings,* Vol. 3, No. 1. Princeton, N.J.: Educational Testing Service, 1976.

Kimmel, E. W. "Financing Credit by Examination: A Framework for Discussion." Princeton, N.J.: Educational Testing Service, 1976. Unpublished paper.

Klees, S. "Post-Secondary Open Learning Systems: Cost, Effectiveness, and Benefit Considerations." *Designed Diversity '75: Conference Proceedings.* Lincoln, Neb.: University of Mid-America, 1975.

Kreplin, Hannah. "Credit by Examination: A Review and Analysis of the Literature." Ford Foundation Report, July 1971, 20 pp.

Losak, J., and T. Lin. "A Comparison of Academic Success between Students Who Earned College Credit via the College-Level Examination Program (CLEP) General Examinations and Those Who Enrolled in Courses." *Journal of Educational Research,* Vol. 67, November 1973, pp. 127–130.

McCluskey, J., and M. J. Richmond. "Summary Report on Arkansas State University's Participation in the CLEP, 1971–75." Arkansas State University, 1975. Unpublished paper.

McElwain, W. J. "Academic Achievement of Students Earning Credit through the College-Level Examination Program General Examinations. Dissertation, Florida Atlantic University, College of Education, 1976.

Meinert, Charles W. "Time-Shortened Degrees," *ERIC Higher Education Research Report,* No. 8. Washington, D.C.: American Association for Higher Education, 1974.

Meyer, P. *Awarding College Credit for Non-College Learning.* San Francisco: Jossey-Bass, 1975.

Moughamian, H. "Financing Credit by Examination: Issues and Implications." City Colleges of Chicago, 1976. Unpublished paper.

Moughamian, H. "A Follow-Up of City Colleges of Chicago Students Earning 24 Semester Hours through the College-Level Examination Program (CLEP)." March 1975.

Nelson, Fred A. "Has the Time Gone for an External Degree?" *Journal of Higher Education,* Vol. 45, March 1974, pp. 174–183.

O'Hearne, J. J. "New College Scholarships: Rewards in the Coin of the Realm." *The College Board Review,* No. 83, Spring 1972, pp. 22–24.

Ozaki, R. H. *CLEP Students Compared to Non-CLEP Students in the Community College.* DeKalb Community College, April 1977.

Radloff, Barbara. "Time Shortening: An Idea Whose Time Has Come— and Gone?" *Carnegie Quarterly,* Vol. 25, Winter 1977, pp. 1–3.

Sharon, Amiel T. "A Model for Awarding College Credit for Work Experience." *Journal of Higher Education,* Vol. 47, November–December 1976, pp. 701–710.

Slygh, W. M., and F. Nelson. "CLEP: Its Impact on Articulation." *College and University*, Vol. 48, Summer 1973, p. 306.

Smart, John M., and Charles Evans. "State Policy-Makers and Time-Shortened Degrees." *Journal of Higher Education*, Vol. 48, March–April 1977, pp. 202–215.

Solmon, Lewis, and Paul Taubman, eds. *Does College Matter?* New York: Academic Press, 1973.

Stark, Joan M. "The Three Year B.A.: Who Will Choose It? Who Will Benefit?" *Journal of Higher Education*, Vol. 44, December 1973, pp. 703–715.

Stecher, C. "CLEP and the Great Credit Giveaway." *Change*, Vol. 9, No. 3, March 1977, pp. 36–43.

Trivett, David A. "Credit for Prior Off-Campus Learning." *ERIC Higher Education Research Report*, No. 2. Washington, D.C.: American Association for Higher Education, 1975.

Wagner, Alan P. "Student Persistence through Postsecondary Education: Patterns, Influences, and Implications for Public Policy Research Proposal." West Lafayette, Ind.: Purdue University, 1977. Mimeographed.

Willingham, W. W. *College Placement and Exemption*. New York: College Entrance Examination Board, 1974.

Yamamoto, K. "Some Comments on Dangers of Credit by Examination." *The Educational Forum*, Vol. 39, No. 3, March 1975, pp. 355–361.

Should examinations for credit be based on
norm-referenced or criterion-referenced testing?

What's a good way to set cutoff scores?

Ernest W. Kimmel received his undergraduate and graduate education at Harvard University. At Educational Testing Service he has been a program director and an area director of college-level placement and equivalence programs. At present he is director of test development for College Board programs. He has published in a number of professional journals and books.

Measurement Considerations in Credit-by-Examination Programs

ERNEST W. KIMMEL

Some unusual measurement problems are presented by the use of examinations to award college credit. The practical application of examinations for granting credit leads to practices that do not fit well the assumptions of either classical test theory (usually called norm-referenced testing) or the more recent criterion-referenced testing model. The way in which student achievement is measured for purposes of awarding college credit must take into account concerns raised by both these testing models while avoiding complete identification with either school of thought.

A brief review of the testing models will highlight both the insights they bring to credit by examination and the assumptions that are at variance with this application of testing.

CLASSICAL TEST THEORY

Classical test theory has its origins in attempts to measure intelligence or aptitude. For over half a century, however, it has also been the conceptual foundation for most efforts to measure students' achievement in specific subjects. This model makes a number of assumptions that are important in considering its application to credit by examination. First, it assumes there is a single underlying trait that is being measured by a given test. For example, a student's score on the verbal sections of the Scholastic Aptitude Test (SAT) represents his or her position on a single dimension or trait of verbal ability. Yet, in the credit-by-examination concept many examinations are modeled on complex courses covering a number of distinct topics that do not fit along a single dimension. For example, can the variety of topics covered in a college chemistry course all be assumed to be part of a single dimension of "chemistry achievement"?

The classical test model also assumes that a primary purpose of a test is to maximize discrimination among individuals — that is, to spread out individuals so that distinctions can be made among them regarding their position on the underlying dimension. In effect, such tests rank test takers from highest to lowest along this dimension. This is an appropriate assumption when the purpose is to choose the "best" candidates for admission to a college. In credit by examination, however, the concern is not usually with the ordering of individuals across a wide range of achievement levels, but rather with determining whether an individual has achieved the performance level in the subject that would be expected of students who receive credit. How far the given student is from the established cutoff score is usually of little interest. That expected standard or performance level is often expressed in terms of the subject content rather than the student's position relative to other students. The purpose is to make a yes or no distinction, not to rank students in order to choose the "best."

The key distinction of classical test theory is that an individual's score derives its meaning from its relationship to the scores of others. A typical norm-referenced attitude is that "it is impossible to set up definite levels or kinds of performance in these pupil aspects [achievement of instructional objectives] without *relating* the performance of pupils one to another" (Remmers, Gage, and Rummel 1965, p. 37). As discussed below, appropriate norms can be useful in establishing standards for awarding credit by examination. Once the standards are established, however, individual scores derive their meaning for credit by examination from their relationship to the standard, not from their relationship to the performance of other students.

Although classical test theory suggests a number of considerations in establishing test validity, in practice the most common tactic has been to demonstrate the examination's usefulness in predicting relative performance in some subsequent educational endeavor. This is not always the most useful tactic for credit by examination. It is one way of validating the examination in a sequentially structured subject, but it is not appropriate in fields where there is no assumption of a sequence between college courses. Of more importance in validating a credit-by-examination instrument is the demonstration that performance on the test is highly related to performance in the course (or other requirement) for which credit is to be given.

CRITERION-REFERENCED TESTING

What, then, of criterion-referenced testing? This *enfant terrible* of the measurement world was first suggested less than two decades ago (Glaser and Klaus 1962). The Advanced Placement Program (APP) was already well under way, and the first editions of the examinations that would make up the College-Level Examination Program (CLEP) were under development. Criterion-referenced testing has developed in the context of measuring the outcomes of instruction. In its initial definition it sought to make scores informative about a student's behavior—that is, what the student can do—rather than, as in norm-referenced testing, the student's position relative to some group of students. By this definition, the items on a criterion-referenced test are tied to a set of behavioral objectives. Some proponents of criterion-referenced testing suggest that the criterion against which the test score is referenced is the cutoff score, or "mastery level" of performance. It seems more useful, however, to interpret this model to mean that a "criterion-referenced test is used to ascertain an individual's status with respect to a well-defined behavioral domain" (Popham 1978a, p. 6); that is, the criterion against which performance is referenced is the defined set of behaviors. Although some proponents of criterion-referenced testing seem to suggest that a passing standard or cutoff score derives automatically from the definition of expected behaviors, in actuality the setting of cutoff scores for criterion-referenced tests is no less judgmental a process than for norm-referenced tests (Glass 1978).

Criterion-referenced tests have been defined by the following four characteristics (Lindvall and Nitko 1975, p. 76):

"1. The classes of behaviors that define different achievement levels are specified as clearly as possible before the test is constructed.

"2. Each behavior class is defined by a set of test situations (that is, test items or test tasks) in which the behaviors and all their important nuances can be displayed.

"3. Given that the classes of behavior have been specified and that the test situations have been defined, a representative sampling plan is designed and used to select the test tasks that will appear on any form of the test.

"4. The obtained score must be capable of being referenced objectively and meaningfully to the individual's performance characteristics in these classes of behavior."

Many aspects of the criterion-referenced model seem attractive to the credit-by-examination situation. Its emphasis on what a student can do, in a particular subject, addresses the concern of many faculty members when faced with decisions about placement or awarding credit.

The criterion-referenced model does, however, have a number of drawbacks to its use as the conceptual basis for designing examinations to be used in awarding credit. First, it presumes a specificity of behavioral objectives or expected outcomes that is rarely found in a college course. Second, a highly specific set of objectives would reduce its applicability across a number of colleges and universities. Third, without a massive analysis of the expected outcomes of the comparable college courses, such an approach could result in standards for earning credit by examination that would be quite different from those for earning credit in a college-taught course.

College courses have rarely been defined in terms of behavioral objectives. Similarly, the examinations for awarding credit that are modeled on college courses have not been constructed in terms of behavioral objectives. One can imagine the difficulty of getting any two faculty members who teach comparable courses to agree on a common set of behavioral objectives for their courses, let alone to agree on a set of test items that would demonstrate a given behavior.

In the rare instance where a college faculty has developed courses based on a behavioral-objectives approach to the curriculum, they probably have developed tests to assess whether students have achieved the specific objectives. These tests could conceivably be used as a basis for awarding credit at that college. In practice, however, one must ask whether anyone who had not been involved in a program of instruction tied to those particular objectives would be able to pass the tests at the expected level. Their very specificity would militate against their use as a means of articulating learning that occurred elsewhere and equating it with the courses at that college.

Similarly, if the objectives measured by an examination are specific enough to fit the criterion-referenced paradigm, it seems unlikely that the examination will be appropriate for use in assessing subject-matter achievement that is creditable at a variety of colleges and universities with differing sets of objectives. The higher education system in the United States encompasses a wide diversity of institutions. Credit by examination must fit within the general pattern of student choice of, and movement among, these institutions. External examinations that are appropriate to only one institution restrict and limit the student's ability to take advantage of the rich diversity of American higher education.

If a test were tied to a specific set of behavioral objectives, it seems likely that teachers would expect credit-by-examination candidates to be proficient at all, or most, objectives without regard to whether there were similar expectations for their in-class students. Without a careful analysis of the objectives of the course, it would be impossible to tell if credit-by-examination students were being held to comparable standards.

EQUIVALENCE AND CONTENT REFERENCING

Although neither the norm-referenced model nor the criterion-referenced model is altogether applicable to credit by examination, each provides a concept that is important to both the development of tests and the establishment of standards for awarding credit. From the norm-referenced tradition comes the notion of equivalency — that credit should be awarded for a level of demonstrated achievement equivalent to that attained by students taking the comparable on-campus course. In practice this has frequently been extended to mean "equivalent to the performance of students in appropriate courses at a variety of colleges and universities."

From the criterion-referenced school comes a renewed emphasis on describing student performance in terms of the content of and the skills in the subject being tested.

The task confronting credit by examination is to achieve the appropriate balance between these two concerns, which come together when a committee of teachers is appointed by the College Board to build an examination for APP or CLEP. Their first task is to define the content and the skills that students taking a similar course at a variety of colleges might be expected to have learned. To augment the committee members' personal experience and knowledge of curriculum practices, they are periodically provided with an analysis of the content of popular textbooks or the results of a survey of a sample of colleges that use the particular examination. In effect, the committee defines a generalized course to serve as a reference point for the examination. This generalized course is probably not identical to the course at any given college, but it includes the topics and skills that are typical of many college courses. The goal of the committee is for this generalized course to be recognized by most colleges as a legitimate variation of a course offered on their campus. In the Advanced Placement Program this generalized course is explicitly described in the course description provided to secondary schools. In CLEP the underlying course is implicit in the description of the examination published for candidates and institutional users. It is important to stress that such a generalized course is not just a compilation of those topics common to most college courses — that is, the lowest common denominator. Rather, it reflects the committee's professional judgment as to the balance of topics and skills to be included in an integral and comprehensive college course.

Similarly, in writing the questions and setting the tasks covered on the examination, the committee seeks to minimize recall of specific details and to emphasize the applications that most teachers would agree are important outcomes of their course.

The committee judgments regarding the appropriateness of content and of questions tapping that content are balanced, typically, with information about the actual student performance on individual questions. This information, gathered through pretesting, may confirm the committee's assessment of the question or lead to the discarding or revision of the question. The test construction process must ensure that the questions posed are appropriate both to the population being tested and to the content of typical college courses.

SETTING INSTITUTIONAL POLICY

The competing concepts of equivalency and content referencing of the test scores should both be involved in the process by which a college or a university sets its credit-by-examination standards. An institution's policy should be defensible both in terms of the level of competency in the subject matter required for credit and in terms of the comparability of the standard of performance required for credit by examination with that required for credit through class enrollment.

Once a college or a university has resolved to have a policy of credit by examination, the first step should be an inward look at the courses or requirements for which such credit might be earned. The faculty members involved should be asked to define the major goals or anticipated outcomes of the course or requirement. For example, if the college has a general education requirement in the humanities, what are the essential skills or understanding that are expected of anyone meeting that requirement on the campus? Should the student be able to associate a specific piece of sculpture with a given period or school, to distinguish among poetic meters, to identify the historical period when a particular musical form was dominant? Without such an effort to define the major outcomes of a course or requirement, the institution has no rational basis for judging whether a given examination is an adequate basis for awarding credit.

After the goals of the on-campus course have been defined, the next step is to decide whether to use a particular examination for awarding credit. One should not, of course, expect to find a 100 percent match between the expected outcomes of the on-campus course and the skills and knowledge tapped by the examination. The appropriate comparison would be between the on-campus course and the "generalized" course underlying the examination. If someone had taken that generalized course on another campus, would transfer credit be allowed at the receiving institution? If the content and skills domain sampled by the examination is similar to the domain covered by the course, the examination should provide an adequate basis for awarding credit — even if a particular edition of the test does not include a question on the department chairman's pet topic.

Assuming that the faculty decides that a particular examination is suitable for awarding credit, the persons charged with implementing a policy of credit by examination are faced with the task of setting the cutoff score or grade for which credit will be given. It should be pointed out that there is no automatic or natural standard for awarding credit. Human judgment is involved in whichever strategy is used for arriving at a standard. The important thing is to avoid capricious judgments — by understanding where, in the process, judgments are being made and by being aware of the values and concerns of those who make the judgments.

There are a number of strategies institutions might follow in setting their standards for awarding credit by examination. The best strategies take into account both measurement models by looking at the content and skills measured by the examination *and* the extent to which students in courses offered by the institution actually acquire the same skills and master the same content. In other words, the best policies are based on judgments that consider both the substance of the examination and the actual performance of on-campus students.

National Standards

The strategy that is easiest for an institution is to adopt a nationally recommended standard. The Advanced Placement Program has carefully established a grade of 3 as meaning a qualified performance in terms of the generalized college course measured by the examination. In APP the judgment is made by the chief reader, who has worked closely with the faculty committee that developed the examination. The chief reader also has carefully analyzed the kind of performance expected on the free-response section of the examination. Through lengthy discussions with committee members and readers, the chief reader has acquired a good sense of what faculty members would expect a qualified student to achieve in terms of the substance of the equivalent college course.

In addition, however, the chief reader has a good deal of information about student performance. Invariably, he or she knows the distribution of raw scores for the current AP candidate group, both on the multiple-choice section and on the several free-response questions. Typically the performance of the current group can be related to those who received grades of 3, 4, and so forth, in previous years. Increasingly, APP has been able to provide the chief reader with information about the performance on the examination of students who took the comparable course at colleges participating in APP. Although this national standard is not tied directly to the performance of on-campus students, an institution that accepts the APP reported grade of 3 as its level for awarding credit can be assured that consideration of both the content of courses and the examination and the quality of student performance has entered into the professional judgment that these students are qualified.

Throughout its history CLEP has tended to put more emphasis on student performance in setting a standard for awarding credit. The original, and now superseded, recommendation of the American Council on Education that the 25th percentile should be the cutoff point for awarding credit for the CLEP General Examinations is rationally defensible within a norm-referenced framework. Given a reference group, all of whose members are "qualified" in the subject matter being tested, it is reasonable to argue that the equivalent treatment would be to give credit to all who scored at or above the lowest person in the qualified referenced group. Denying credit to the bottom 25 percent appears to be a conservative step in this framework. The disagreement comes in judging whether all members of the actual reference group can be considered qualified. The failure of this normative recommendation to consider the level of substantive mastery indicated by this score level has generated considerable faculty criticism. The recommendations regarding the Subject Examinations, where the suggested standard for credit has been tied to the grades earned by a sample of college students, have been more readily accepted.

The College-Level Examination Program is now in the process of working out a new procedure for arriving at a national recommendation of a range of so-called qualified scores. The new procedure asks a faculty panel to combine its judgments about substantive competence with information about the performance of a sample of students. New recommendations for the General Examinations, along with a description of the processes followed by the faculty panels, are expected by the end of 1979. Thus, institutions using CLEP will have available a national standard that considers both content and student performance.

In addition to minimizing work for an institution, the use of national (or statewide) standards has a great advantage for students: A common standard across institutions enhances the transferability of the credit earned by examination as a student moves from one college to another.

A major obstacle to the development and use of national standards, however, is the increasing reluctance of colleges, faculty members, and students to cooperate in collecting relevant information about student performance. While many institutions want to use information based on a representative sample of students in similar colleges, the decreasing willingness by faculty and students to cooperate for the general good has seriously hampered efforts to provide student data useful in setting standards for awarding credit by examination. The College Board, ETS, or any other agency needs to operate in consort with education institutions. They cannot provide quality measurement programs without cooperation.

Local Standards

A substantial number of colleges, for a variety of reasons, choose to set a standard that is not tied to a national recommendation. Setting aside the possibility of manipulating a college's credit-by-examination policy to enhance its competitive advantage in this time of declining enrollments, how can a college approach this decision? Again, the preferable strategy involves the combination of faculty expectations regarding the content to be mastered with information about student performance.

One way of getting faculty members to define operationally their expectations in terms of subject-matter mastery is to ask a panel of faculty members, ideally those teaching the relevant course, to go through the examination item by item. A number of procedures for item-by-item judgments have been suggested in the measurement literature (Nedelsky 1954; Ebel 1972, 1978; Angoff 1971). For each question these procedures require a judgment expressed in such terms as the probability of a "qualified" student's passing the item; or the number of distractors that a minimally qualified student could identify as incorrect; or the number of items judged as "essential." A limited amount of algebraic manipulation of the resulting judgments leads to an estimate of a passing score.

The next step is to compare this estimate of a passing score with the test performance of a relevant group of students. Ideally this group would be composed of students who had been instructed by the same faculty members who make the item-by-item judgments. Such a comparison would demonstrate whether the faculty members were realistic in their judgments.

Other groups of students could be used in comparing faculty judgments with student performance — for example, students at the same institution who took the relevant course but were not instructed by members of the faculty panel. The student performance data might be drawn from other comparable institutions or from reference data provided by the testing program involved.

The standard derived from faculty judgments and the student data can be related formally through a decision-theory model. Such an approach allows the institution to estimate the proportion of classification errors that it would make at a given standard or cutoff score; that is, how many "qualified" (deserving of credit) students would be denied credit if our standard were set at x? And how many "unqualified" students would receive credit at this level?

Any classification practice will have these two types of errors. Also, the number of false negatives will increase when the number of false positives is decreased, and vice versa. The use of a formal model enables the institution to analyze the impact of a proposed standard on a known student population. Furthermore, the institution can assign relative values to these two types of classification errors. If it is more important to prevent "unqualified" students from receiving credit than to be sure that "qualified" students do receive credit, one raises the cutoff score.

This approach can be illustrated by the hypothetical data in Table 1. The sample institution has decided that everyone who received A, B, or C in Study Skills 101 should be considered qualified, while everyone who received D or E should be considered unqualified. All participants in the course were tested with the proposed examination for credit, and the resulting score distribution is shown in Table 1.

Table 1
Distribution of Scores for Students in Study Skilis 101

Test Scores	Qualified (Students earning A, B, or C)	Unqualified (Students earning D or E)
60 and above	36	—
58–59	15	2
56–57	27	1
54–55	45	4
52–53	51	3
50–51	57	15
48–49	36	23
46–47	15	20
44–45	9	25
43 and below	9	7
Total	300	100

If the item-by-item judgments of a faculty panel suggested that scores of 54 and above qualify a student for credit, only 41 percent of the qualified students would receive credit, along with 7 percent of the unqualified. If one looked at the actual numbers involved, such a policy would deny credit to 177 "qualified" students while granting credit to 7 "unqualified" students.

If, on the other hand, the institution wanted the proportion of qualified and unqualified students misclassified to be about equal, the passing score would be set at 50. This would result in 23 percent of the qualified students' being refused credit while 25 percent of the unqualified students were mistakenly granted credit. It should be reemphasized that even with this decision-theory model a sizable element of judgment is called for. The point at which the number of misclassifications is minimized is not necessarily the point at which the passing score should be set. A judgment must be made regarding the relative importance of each type of classification error. This model provides no more than a means of estimating the likelihood of each type of error. It provides a means of estimating the impact on a known group of students of a proposed credit-by-examination policy. The proposed policy may have been arrived at by the item-by-item judgments of a faculty panel, by following the example of similar colleges, or by some other means. The interplay between student performance and faculty judgments about content would seem to lead to a more reasonable and defensible policy than one based on either set of data alone.

FOLLOW-UP

Setting a credit-by-examination policy is not a onetime enterprise. As has been pointed out in other papers, an institution periodically needs to review its policy to determine if it continues to be appropriate. Although there are many aspects of subsequent student behavior of interest to an institution, I suggest that one relates to what was defined as the institution's first task in developing a policy—namely, a review of the expected outcomes of the course for which credit by examination is to be allowed. If the outcomes measured by the examination are similar to those of the on-campus course, credit-by-examination students who take subsequent courses in the field should perform at least at the same level as those who received credit by passing the equivalent course. If an empirical study supports this expectation, it can be assumed that the match between the course and the examination is a reasonable one. If the credit-by-examination students perform more poorly than do the on-campus students in subsequent courses, the institution must determine if essential elements are missing from the examination. Conversely, when the credit-by-examination students do far better, are they being asked to demonstrate achievement of outcomes not demanded of the students whose credit came through course work?

In this paper I have argued that the use of examinations to award college credit does not fit well the assumptions of either measurement model in current use. Both the norm-referenced model and the criterion-referenced model do, however, raise major concerns that must be dealt with in both the construction of the examinations and the implementation of a credit-by-examination policy at a college. These twin concerns focus on maintaining a defensible level of subject-matter competency while setting expectations that are comparable to those for students enrolled in the appropriate courses.

BIBLIOGRAPHY

Angoff, W. H. "Scales, Norms and Equivalent Scores," in R. L. Thorndike, ed., *Educational Measurement,* 2d ed. Washington, D.C.: American Council on Education, 1971.

Ebel, R. L. "The Case for Norm-Referenced Measurements." *Educational Researcher,* Vol. 7, No. 11, 1978, pp. 3–5.

Ebel, R. L. *Essentials of Educational Measurement.* Englewood Cliffs, N.J.: Prentice-Hall, 1972.

Glaser, R., and D. J. Klaus. "Proficiency Measurement: Assessing Human Performance, in R. M. Gagne, ed., *Psychological Principles in Systems Development.* New York: Holt, Rinehart & Winston, 1962.

Glass, G. V. "Standards and Criteria." *Journal of Educational Measurement,* Vol. 15, 1978, pp. 237–261.

Hambleton, R. K., H. Swaminathan, J. Algina, and D. B. Coulson. "Criterion-Referenced Testing and Measurement: A Review of Technical Issues and Developments." *Review of Educational Research,* Vol. 48, 1978, pp. 1–47.

Lindvall, C. M., and A. J. Nitko. *Measuring Pupil Achievement and Aptitude,* 2d ed. New York: Harcourt Brace Jovanovich, 1975.

Linn, R. L. "Demands, Cautions, and Suggestions for Setting Standards." *Journal of Educational Measurement,* Vol. 15, 1978, pp. 301–308.

Meskauskas, J. A. "Evaluation Models for Criterion-Referenced Testing:

Views Regarding Mastery and Standard Setting." *Review of Educational Research,* Vol. 46, 1976, pp. 133–158.

Messick, S. "The Standard Problem: Meaning and Values in Measurement and Evaluation." *American Psychologist,* Vol. 30, 1975, pp. 955–966.

Nedelsky, L. "Absolute Grading Standards for Objective Tests." *Educational and Psychological Measurement,* Vol. 14, 1954, pp. 3–19.

Popham, W. J. "The Case for Criterion-Referenced Measurements." *Educational Researcher,* Vol. 7, No. 11, 1978, pp. 6–10.

Popham, W. J. *Criterion-Referenced Measurement.* Englewood Cliffs, N.J.: Prentice-Hall, 1978.

Remmers, H. H., N. L. Gage, and J. F. Rummel. *A Practical Introduction to Measurement and Evaluation,* 2d ed. New York: Harper & Row, 1965.

At the colloquium Douglas R. Whitney, of the American Council on Education's Office on Educational Credit and Credentials, was asked to respond to Ernest W. Kimmel's paper. Mr. Whitney's remarks were expanded into the following paper on "Considerations in Setting Standards for Credit-by-Examination Programs."

My remarks are more an elaboration of some of Dr. Kimmel's points related to setting cutoff scores for credit awards than a reaction to, or criticism of, the measurement considerations he outlined. My focus is on setting standards—identifying the minimum test score level(s) required to earn credit at an institution. This is a troublesome aspect of current credit-by-examination programs, especially when standards are being set for examinations developed by "external" agencies (for example, the College Board, the American College Testing Program, and the Defense Activity for Nontraditional Education Support).

At the outset I should identify a personal prejudice. The American Council on Education's Commission on Educational Credit and Credentials recommended (at a meeting in December 1978) that such standards reflect a degree of equity between the standards used by institutions in awarding credit based on test results and those used in awarding credit for courses completed under the auspices of other education institutions (transfer credit). The principle of equity also argues that standards set for credit-by-examination programs should reflect levels of student achievement comparable with those demonstrated by students completing local courses with a grade that is just sufficient to earn credit at the institution. It should be understood, of course, that the skills and knowledge reflected in the test and in the course must also be comparable in kind and in difficulty.

The commission's recommendation can be stated as follows: *Standards for awarding credit on the basis of examination results should neither demand significantly more nor accept significantly less from students seeking credit on this basis than is required of students earning credit by completing local courses.*

I find this position entirely acceptable, but those who do not may find themselves less concerned (or more concerned),with the observations that follow. The position, however, seems entirely consistent with that of the College Board.[1]

FACULTY ROLE IN SETTING STANDARDS

Most technical specialists (psychometricians) and most faculty would probably agree that the primary consideration in setting standards should be the judgments of qualified and experienced teachers, based on reviews of the test specifications and questions and of the prevailing standards in similar courses or programs at the institution. Some problems arise, however, in carrying out these recommendations.

Can faculty reviewers discharge this responsibility with sufficient concern for the concept of equity? If the examination for which a standard is being set was developed especially to reflect local course objectives, if it was planned and written by local faculty, and if it was administered to students completing local courses, the answer would have to be "of course," since that is precisely what occurs in the conventional setting—whether the instructional activities take place on campus or through correspondence or extension programs. For a CLEP Subject Examination, however, the course "syllabus" reflected in the test design is a generalized one that does not necessarily match any single existing course. The test questions were developed by a committee of experienced and qualified faculty from a small number of *other* campuses, and the tests were administered to students completing courses at a number of *other* campuses. Each of these "differences" can limit the ability of faculty reviewers to establish equitable standards.

During the past year the American Council on Education has assembled more than 30 teams of experienced and qualified faculty to review tests developed for use in credit-by-examination programs. For one series of 14 test reviews, these teams established minimum score recommendations for awarding college-level credit, based on their experience in teaching courses with content similar to that of the tests, a thorough review of the test questions, and an analysis of the distribution of test scores for students completing related courses at a number of institutions. In every case the recommendations were so high to have denied credit to more than half the students who had actually taken the courses and earned credit; often as many as 60 percent of those completing the course would have failed to qualify for credit based on examination results. While this is not sufficient to establish a conclusive case for an upward bias in these recommended standards, it is sufficient to cause some concern. My conclusion, based on direct involvement with 16 such recent reviews, is that it is very difficult for faculty members to examine a test constructed by others and recognize the degree of challenge and subtlety — and, occasionally, ambiguity — reflected in the questions. If I am correct, this tendency would lead to standards that are unreasonably high.

Are there other acceptable sources for faculty recommendations? In the development of tests such as those in CLEP and other reputable series, the test development committees play a role that is, on a national scale, analogous to the role of the local faculty in the conventional setting. Because the committee members have defined the generalized syllabus to which the test is developed and have usually contributed or revised the test questions (both processes typically involve spirited discussions among committee members), they appear to be in a position to offer helpful advice in setting standards. I would encourage the College Board and other agencies responsible for test development to ask test committees to develop recommendations on standards before new tests and new editions of existing tests are released.

Should a local faculty review always be conducted? Although a local faculty review is recommended for any externally developed examination used for credit awards, there are circumstances in which such a review seems an unwise use of institutional resources. Suppose that at a particular institution an individual student requests an evaluation of his or her results on a test not previously reviewed or administered locally. It is possible, in such a circumstance, to conduct a full local review and test administration in order to develop equitable local standards. But consider the faculty effort required for a thorough review (for example, two or three faculty members devoting three to five hours each to a thorough analysis of the test content and specific test items). Then add the time involved for, say, 30 to 50 students to complete the examination. Because such administrations are often scheduled during a regular class period or two, instructional time may also be sacrificed. This seems to me too dear a price to pay for the ability to make a sound credit decision for a few students.

One unacceptable alternative to an extensive local review is to routinely deny credit awards based on all externally developed examinations except for those that are well known to faculty. A more desirable alternative is to rely on the recommendations of other qualified faculty who have already conducted such reviews. This permits a reasonable credit award to the individual, if deserved, and the resources that would have been required for an extensive local review or administration can be devoted to other tests more frequently presented for credit evaluation. Subsequent progress of individuals receiving credit on the basis of external recommendations can be studied. The success, or lack of it, in subsequent local courses by the first few students receiving credit on this basis reflects on the appropriateness of the original externally recommended standard. Such an approach is very much in the spirit of relying on colleagues' judgments as reflected in the general acceptance of transfer credit from accredited institutions.

NORMATIVE DATA IN SETTING STANDARDS

It is also a long-standing recommendation of education associations and professional psychometricians that the actual test results for an appropriate sample of examinees play a role in setting equitable standards for examination-based credit awards. Often it is especially informative to consider the average test scores or the success rate demonstrated on the test by students who have satisfactorily completed a course with content, objectives, and level similar to those reflected in the test's generalized syllabus. This seems as true for tests whose approach can be considered criterion-referenced as it does for those considered norm-referenced.

In the discussion that follows I have assumed that the content and specific items on the tests are fixed and are no longer subject to alteration—that is, any pretesting data have already been studied and have been used to develop the "final" test form(s)—and that an appropriate faculty review has concluded the tests are relevant, current, and valid. If these steps have not all been completed, normative data are largely irrelevant.

What role should normative data play in setting standards? The principle of equity in credit awards offers a clear role for normative studies in setting standards: The standard should reflect an achievement level similar to that demonstrated by students who satisfactorily complete comparable courses. Even if an initial judgment about standards is made by faculty reviewers, the test results for an appropriate group of such students represent the empirical validation of the original judgment. If original faculty judgments have been reasonably sound, the normative data will offer confirmatory support; if not, the data will register a clear need for adjustment.

If, for example, the original judgments have resulted in a standard that is too high, too few students who complete comparable courses satisfactorily will earn test scores that would have qualified them for credit. Conversely, an initially low standard will permit too many students who do not complete such courses to earn test scores that would have qualified them for credit. Without such data, the judgments are only informed, but unsubstantiated, estimates—not a sufficient basis, in my view, for credit awards.

Dr. Kimmel notes, and my experiences confirm, that it is very difficult to obtain the cooperation of institutional officials and individual faculty in administering new tests and in developing appropriate normative data for such tests. Although it has probably always been difficult to arrange such participation, it appears to have become even more so in recent years. Two reasons for an institution's refusing to participate in such projects are readily understood and can be recognized as legitimate faculty concerns: (1) Such requests for testing are often received after the course in question has been planned. Ideally, such requests would arrive during the previous term, well before the course schedule is determined. (2) The request is made that the tests be administered to all students during a period that might otherwise have been used for instruction, review, or final course assessment. These conditions are desirable because they help ensure the representativeness of the normative results and help provide adequate incentive for the examinees to take the task seriously. Obviously, however, the "costs" associated with allocating class meeting time to this activity are not to be taken lightly; the immediate "benefits" of participation are often neither clear nor substantial.

Other reasons given by institutions for their refusal to participate are also understandable, if less defensible. Two of these are perceptions that can be expressed as follows: (1) Such a request is just like all the other requests that seek permission for enrolled students to take part in research projects or to complete opinion-of-teaching forms; that seek a captive audience to promote institutional and extracurricular activities; that plead for cooperation in enforcing institutional policies on such matters as safety and honesty. (2) Any practice that may result in credit awards on a basis other than completion of the local course is either an inexpensive alternative to rigorous study with the instructor or a threat to reduce the number of student credit hours attributed to the college, department, division, or individual in the institutional scheme for accountability.

The first of these perceptions represents a failure to note that credit-by-examination procedures can result in the award of academic credit. Such awards have long been a faculty responsibility, and rightly so. But pervasive refusals to participate in activities that ensure that such examinations are valid and have appropriate standards will lead either to the failure to meet the needs of students who have become qualified by noninstitutional experiences or to an abrogation of responsibility for setting credit award standards to others (for example, legislators, administrators, test development agencies) who may believe that such programs are desirable.

The second perception cited above is equally shortsighted. Credit-by-examination programs may indeed fail to be creditable alternatives to traditional course activities; they are, however, more likely to develop in this direction from an absence, rather than an excess, of faculty and student involvement. Heavy reliance on such artificial, convenient but narrow indicators as "student credit hours generated" is hardly worth deriding; but if such indices also fail to reflect the considerable faculty energy necessary to evaluate properly the qualifications of students whose learning has been outside institutional sponsorship, they are even less defensible.

In my view, faculty responsibilities for ensuring the validity of instruction and of credit awards for institutionally sponsored courses should be interpreted to include responsibility for reviewing tests intended for use in credit-by-examination programs and for assisting in the development of appropriate normative information on promising tests. Even though the immediate benefits of such activities to individual faculty members or to students currently enrolled in courses are often small, the benefits to future students and to colleagues of valid and efficient means for evaluating extrainstitutional learning are substantial. Although an individual faculty member or a particular group of students should not be expected to contribute an inordinate amount of energy and time to this activity, it does seem reasonable to expect each to participate at least once or twice during their respective teaching careers and enrollments.

How should normative data be used in setting standards? Many technical specialists believe that a comparison of test scores earned by students who complete appropriate courses — with grades or other indicators of learning — is a logical and useful part of the standard-setting process. In an externally developed examination, it is not reasonable to expect a perfect correspondence between the rankings or evaluations on the two sources of information. No test is perfectly reliable, so any set of test results contains the scores of some individuals who may have been more accurately measured by locally developed assessment methods than by the externally developed test. Since locally developed measures are also not perfectly reliable, some disagreements in rankings or evaluations arise from this source as well. On occasion, imperfections in local assessment methods can be expected to account for more of the "errors" in credit decisions than does the externally developed test. Also, because an externally developed test draws on a generalized course syllabus, local differences in emphasis, content, and vocabulary virtually guarantee that evaluations of student learning based on the two sources will never exactly coincide. My observation, however, is that sections of the same local courses taught by different faculty members sometimes show more extreme curricular differences than those between a course and an externally developed examination.

Still, where a test is judged to be substantially related to local course objectives and where standards have appropriately been set, the following statements should be true:

1. Most students who complete a course with an achievement level on local assessment devices sufficient to merit institutional credit awards should earn test scores at or above the set standard.

2. Most students who fail to demonstrate an achievement level on local assessment methods that warrants credit for completing the course should earn test scores below the standard set for the externally developed test.

Evidence that neither occurs suggests that the judgment of test-to-course similarity is in error or that the test, the local assessment methods, or both, are not very reliable. Evidence that one, but not both, of these results occurs suggests that the standards are inappropriate. Some data from Dr. Kimmel's paper (see his Table 1) will be used to illustrate an approach to analyzing the latter situation.

In his data Dr. Kimmel has identified students as either "qualified" (those earning grades of A, B, or C in the course) or "unqualified" (those earning grades of D or E). His data are artificial and are not reported in a way that makes it possible to calculate the most appropriate correlation coefficient between test scores and course grades, but it appears that a coefficient of about $r = .40$ would have resulted if this could have been done. This relatively low value raises some questions about the similarity of course and test content and the degree of reliability of one or another of the assessment methods. Consequently these data show a greater number of inconsistent decisions than might typically be expected in an actual setting.

To illustrate clearly the role that normative data can play in evaluating judgmental standards, consider the consequences of

Table 1

Qualified Examinees (if test score of 54
or better is required for qualification)

| | Test Result | | |
Course Result	Qualified	Not Qualified	Total
Qualified	123	177	300
Not Qualified	10	90	100
Total	133	267	400

an a priori judgment by faculty that a test score of 54 or better is needed for a student to qualify for a credit award (see my Table 1). The scores and grades can be used to locate each person in one of four "cells."

At least two conclusions can be drawn from Table 1:

1. While 300 of the 400 students (75 percent) were judged to be qualified on the basis of course grades, only 133 (33.25 percent) would have been so judged from test results if a test score of 54 or better is required. Immediately, this suggests, but does not prove, that this judgmental standard may be too high.

2. Although it is true that most students whose grades led to an evaluation of "not qualified" earned test scores below the proposed standard (90 percent would have failed to earn credit based on this standard), it is not true that most students judged to be qualified on the basis of course grades earned test scores at or above the proposed standard (only 123 of 300, or 41 percent, did so).

As Dr. Kimmel notes, it is not always desirable to set test standards so that the total *number* of examinees judged as qualified on one basis but unqualified on the other is at a minimum. It may be useful, however, to consider the standard that would be necessary in order to make approximately equal the *percentages* of those qualified by grades, but unqualified by test results, and of those unqualified by grades, but qualified by test results. By experimenting with possible test score standards, it can be seen

Table 2

Qualified Examinees (if test score of 50
or better is required for qualification)

	Test Result		
Course Result	Qualified	Not Qualified	Total
Qualified	231	69	300
Not Qualified	38	62	100
Total	269	131	400

that a test score of 50 or above represents a standard that is as close to this solution as the data permit. Table 2 rearranges the data to illustrate this approach.

If this standard is used, 77 percent of students identified as qualified by course grades (231 of 300) earned test scores high enough to be awarded "deserved" credit; 62 percent of those with inadequate course grades failed to earn test scores high enough to qualify for credit awards (62 of 100). (The "error rates" were, thus, 23 percent not qualifying for "deserved" credit and 38 percent qualifying for "undeserved" credit.)

Although the method for evaluating or adjusting test standards illustrated in Table 2 is not necessarily the most desirable one, it can be used to demonstrate my concluding point:

Any decision about setting test standards for determining credit awards carries an implicit value judgment about the relative seriousness of denying credit to deserving examinees as contrasted with that of awarding credit to undeserving examinees. Such value judgments are better made explicit and discussed openly than ignored or hidden beneath the mantles of "rigorous standards" or "benefit of the doubt."

It is possible to employ a variety of elegant procedures for quantifying such values,[2] for using the results in "solving" for the best standard,[3] and for incorporating the values relevant to society.[4] Interested readers are encouraged to review this problem in light of the contexts set by Willingham[5] and by Hills.[6] In the end, however, the simple display (Table 1 and Table 2) that would result from alternative test score standards puts the issue in its clearest form.

Even if normative data are used in this way, faculty judgments are still paramount. The bases used above for negotiating a proper standard still reflect the course-based evaluations of the faculty (reflected in course grades in Dr. Kimmel's illustration) and the judgments of the relative seriousness of "errors" that should reflect professional judgments by the faculty and others. The use of normative data in this manner does not deny or circumvent traditional and proper faculty responsibilities in these matters. The absence of normative data, however, leaves the faculty judgments without the support (or refutation) that could usually be readily gained. For externally developed tests, normative data provided by the test developer can be used in exactly the same way as local data can if appropriate information on course grades or outcomes is gathered and made available to institutions for study. I encourage the College Board and other test development agencies to provide enough information to permit such analyses; I encourage institutions to use this information to seek equitable and economical solutions to the problem of setting standards on externally developed examinations.

NOTES

1. *Guidelines on the Uses of College Board Test Scores and Related Data.* New York: College Entrance Examination Board, 1977.

2. M. R. Novick and D. V. Lindley, "The Use of More Realistic Utility Functions in Educational Applications." *Journal of Educational Measurement,* Vol. 15, 1978, pp. 181–191.

3. G. V. Glass, "Standards and Criteria." *Journal of Educational Measurement,* Vol. 15, 1978, pp. 237–261.

4. N. W. Burton, "Societal Standards." *Journal of Educational Measurement,* Vol. 15, 1978, pp. 263–271.

5. W. W. Willingham, *College Placement and Exemption.* New York: College Entrance Examination Board, 1974.

6. J. R. Hills, "Use of Measurement in Selection and Placement," in R. L. Thorndike, ed., *Educational Measurement,* 2d ed. Washington, D.C.: American Council on Education, 1971.

Is credit by examination here to stay?

What were the concerns of participants in the colloquium?

Lorrin Kennamer received his doctorate at George Peabody College for Teachers of Vanderbilt University in 1952 and is now dean of the College of Education at the University of Texas at Austin. A professor of geography and education, he has written several geography textbooks, has been associated with a number of scholarly journals, and is coeditor of a series of four college-level monographs in regional geography. Mr. Kennamer is a past chairman of the Board of Trustees of the College Board and was chairman of the National Commission on Performance-Based Teacher Education, American Association of Colleges of Teacher Education.

Prospects for Credit by Examination

LORRIN KENNAMER

Processes and procedures for awarding credit in higher education in this country have not undergone major change since the turn of the century, when Harvard established the elective system. It is easy to believe the primary reliance on course completion to fulfill degree requirements, particularly in the undergraduate years, has been practiced so long that it is the only way we have ever proceeded.

A PERSPECTIVE

Our current scene is a well-organized, systematic, sequential system: kindergarten to elementary school to junior high to secondary school to community or baccalaureate college and then to professional school. As Baird Whitlock states in his book, however, we had great diversity in the early days of higher education in this country. ". . . it is perhaps fitting to remember that two hundred years ago at Phillips Academy in Andover, Massachusetts, Josiah Quincy of Boston, aged 6, was a classmate of James Anderson of Londonderry, New Hampshire, aged 30. . . .

"So diverse were the possibilities in England in the 17th century that William Penn's friend . . . entered his law studies at the Middle Temple at 13 and was called to the bar in the usual seven years, at age 20. . . .

"The pattern in early America was equally diverse. Cotton Mather graduated from Harvard at 16, as did Jonathan Edwards from Yale. John Trumbull left Master Tisdale's school in Lebanon, Connecticut, in 1768 to enter Harvard when he was 12, having completed a course of study that ranged from Greek and Latin to surveying and navigation. In the middle of the 19th century Henry Adams entered Harvard at 16 as an average student, if we

139

are to believe his own estimate of his intellectual powers or his rank in class."[1]

Whitlock says that the keynote of those times was "flexibility based on individual abilities." Shortly after its founding in 1784, the New York Board of Regents determined that college students did not have to enter as freshmen, but would be admitted to classes for which they were qualified.

The educational setting became more formal with the rise of the academies and the introduction of the land-grant schools. The academies disappeared; some became colleges and some became high schools, often with confusing overlap. To achieve standardization in the years that followed, the reports of the Committee of Ten and a committee of the National Education Association established college entrance requirements that included certain constants in all secondary schools. The Carnegie Foundation for the Advancement of Teaching added to the conformity when it "defined 'college' in terms of the academic units required for admission. The bookkeeping system known as Carnegie units took over the role of defining high school–college articulation. . . . By 1930 the entire structure was firmly in place and hallowed as tradition."[2]

Higher education in the United States moved from an original pattern of dissimilarity in admissions procedures, age of students, and degree practices in the 1700s and 1800s to standard and set practices in the 1900s. Since the enactment of the Education Amendments of 1972, the use of the term "higher education" has shifted to the term "postsecondary education." Higher education is limited to curriculums that lead to degrees, whereas postsecondary education, the dominant term today, is appropriately used when it applies to the many educational opportunities available to post-high-school-age adults. The press for greater flexibility and variety in educational opportunity is recognized. The many discussions of nontraditional education are known to us all. These changes are coming not in a broad, uniform flow but in a series of

1. Baird W. Whitlock, *Don't Hold Them Back*. New York: College Entrance Examination Board, 1978, pp. 4–5.
2. Ibid., pp. 9–10.

what seem at times to be disjointed activities by many groups. There appears to be a central theme, however, in the discussions of future possible changes in higher education: the concept of credit by examination.

We have said that the first era of higher education in this country was one of diversity, followed by the second era of standardized format and procedure. We are now entering the third era, which may result in more flexibility within the system — as illustrated by the claims made for credit by examination.

Our educational establishment is feeling pressures for change. What we might call "social-educational inventions" are beginning to cause stresses and strains in our formalized higher education pattern. The list that follows illustrates some of the developments leading to change in the traditional classroom practice of semester hour credits.

1930s	Statement by University of Chicago of requirements in terms of educational attainments
1932	Locally developed evaluation procedures in University of Buffalo program for superior high school students
1940s	United States Armed Forces Institute (USAFI)
1945	Commission on the Accreditation of Service Experiences (CASE) of American Council on Education
1955	Advanced Placement Program of the College Board
1961	College Proficiency Examination Program (CPEP) of Board of Regents of State of New York
1965	Comprehensive College Tests of Educational Testing Service (ETS)
1966	College-Level Examination Program (CLEP) of the College Board
1968	Definition by National Task Force of Continuing Education Unit (CEU)
1970	Regents External Degree (RED) of State of New York
1971	Commission on Nontraditional Study of the College Board and ETS
1974	Establishment by American Council on Education of Program on Non-Collegiate-Sponsored Instruction
1975	American Council on Education: New program on Evaluation of Learning Associated with Occupa-

tional Competency (Army enlisted Military Occupational Specialties [MOS] evaluated)

1976   American College Testing Program Proficiency Examination (PEP)

1978   American Council on Education: Credit Recommendations for Nationally Registered Apprentice Training Programs

Organizational Efforts

DANTES: Defense Activity for Nontraditional Educational Support

OEC: Office on Educational Credit of American Commission on Education

CAEL: Cooperative Assessment of Experiential Learning

NOCTI: National Occupational Competency Testing Institute

AUEC: Association of University Evening Colleges

V-TECS: Voc-Tech Education Consortium of States in Southern Association of Colleges and Schools

Guides by American Council on Education:

Guide to the Evaluation of Educational Experiences in the Armed Services (4th ed., 1976)

The National Guide to Credit Recommendations for Non-Collegiate Courses (1974)

No one of the events is of great significance alone, but the sequence of activities emanating from various areas of our society suggests that higher education, as we have known it, should develop more flexible procedures for admissions and for credentials. Credit by examination is here to stay. It can call upon history for precedents and can be a vehicle for future change. It has many traditions from which to choose.

PROBLEMS OF THE MOMENT

Because credit has been awarded by examination for a number of years, it is feasible to reexamine the concept. For that reason, about 150 high school and college faculty and administrators gathered in March 1979 in Madison, Wisconsin, for a national invitational colloquium to consider issues related to this form of credit. Focus was on the educational significance at both the high school and the college levels. This meant considering issues related to the Advanced Placement Program (APP) and the College-Level Examination Program (CLEP). The sponsoring agencies believed the time had come for a review.

It is no surprise that much of the discussion and many of the concerns at the colloquium were focused on the College-Level Examination Program, which was originally designed for adults returning to college with uncredited educational experiences. The adults had gained their knowledge on the job, in home study, or via educational television. As the program progressed through the years, however, a surprising development was that many thousands of newly graduated high school seniors took the CLEP General Examinations and gained the equivalent of six hours of college credit at well over 1,000 colleges and universities. It should be noted that the concerns focused more on the General Examinations than on the Subject Examinations.

The following statements are from high school and college CLEP participants:

☐ There need to be guidelines for the use and interpretation of CLEP.

☐ There is doubt about the total educational experience of a young student who, after one semester as a freshman, can then become a junior because of successful scores on the General Examinations as well as the Subject Examinations.

☐ If people in higher education are going to be expected to grant credit for comparable or nearly comparable examinations, there must be some sort of equation in the scores.

☐ There is some danger in faculty noninvolvement in these examinations.

☐ The departments usually set AP standards, and the administration sets CLEP standards, which are usually lower.

☐ There is a basic faculty distrust of CLEP, since the General Examinations test nothing comparable to course work. The College Board should reinforce its position and thinking regarding the purposes of CLEP, the group for which it was designed, and how it should be used.

☐ The College Board has to recognize that they have created CLEP to serve a certain group. When it is used for that purpose, it achieves its goal; as it is used, it raises serious educational questions.

The colloquium participants expressed equal concern regarding the relationships between CLEP and APP. The College Board has developed the two examination programs for different times and for different purposes. APP, designed for certain high school populations, has been moving along very well as a college-level program with a high school locale. CLEP, comprising General Examinations and Subject Examinations, focuses on the adult who seeks credit for informal learning, and the credit is applied to a degree program on a campus. There is no question that confusion has arisen because of the overlap between these two programs. Members of the colloquium stated the following:

☐ If two tests are necessary, there should be a clearer definition of each test and more guidance on the use of each.

☐ Taking CLEP at a time considered unwise — that is, taking the examinations in high school and then not taking Advanced Placement Program courses — causes damage to the APP.

☐ Although both programs are good, the differences in equating the two scores need attention.

☐ There is concern whether someone who could pass CLEP for credit has had the same quality of training or learning as someone who has taken AP.

☐ AP is scored differently and has a better reputation with the faculty, while CLEP is the new kid on the block and the faculty is not sure of its objectives.

☐ Some educators believe their students usually gain more credit from CLEP than from a comparable score on AP, and, as a result, fewer students are taking AP examinations.

☐ The College Board should correlate the types of examinations that are given so that students do not have to pay additional money to take several examinations.

☐ There seems to be a division between secondary schools committed to APP (and the curriculum) and colleges and universities that use CLEP or other testing procedures. Because the subject tests of CLEP are like the objective part of APP, the equation of these two is not so difficult as the equation of AP examinations and CLEP General Examinations.

The debate between CLEP and APP stems from a basic difference in philosophy as to what credit stands for. One point of view is that it measures achievement in accordance with a set syllabus. Others would say that credit should also record the educational experience as an interaction involving teacher and student, classroom environment, and peer support and competition.

How well credit by examination can properly evaluate work in humanities courses is an old concern and yet one that continues to raise potent questions. Can machine-scored equivalence tests be suitable for general, or liberal, education? One person pointed out that such examinations might neglect the process, essential to any education, of raising fundamental questions and teaching students to use investigative resources and methods to explore suitable educational questions. Colloquium participants articulated the following difficulties:

☐ Problems are presented in humanities courses whose content can not be readily quantified and tested.

☐ Credit by examination may be suitable in a science course but not for students in a literature course, who are involved in a thinking-feeling experience that requires a more complex response.

☐ Tests seem to be designed to measure the accumulation of knowledge, while courses in literature, art, and philosophy aim at the development of thinking-feeling skills. Is there a test to evaluate these skills? If students take sufficient CLEP examinations, it is possible for them to miss all the humanities requirements and thus an important part of the total educational experience.

☐ In the humanities there is a bigger problem of dealing with intrinsic qualities that can not perhaps be judged on an objective examination.

☐ There is the example of the six-year combined bachelor of arts and M.D. degree. Because of heavy pressure to pass the basic science component of the medical boards, many students opt to CLEP out of general degree courses. This means that humanities and selected social sciences are cut from this program and the student's experience. This does not seem to be the purpose for which CLEP was designed, but it is clearly a use to which it has been put. A suggestion would be to restrict CLEP to clientele it was originally designed to serve: returning adult learners.

Concerns expressed in the previous paragraphs are not new. Economic implications for high schools and colleges, however, are a new concern arising from enrollment reductions at both secondary and postsecondary levels. It is one thing for a faculty member to ascertain the educational viability of credit by examination in a philosophical sense. It is quite another matter if the faculty member believes a major acceptance of such credits might decrease courses taken on campus to the extent that the size of the faculty is reduced. It would not be a surprise, therefore, if there are some reassessments of campus policy regarding how liberal the credit-by-examination practices should be. The following points were made at the colloquium:

☐ If secondary schools are forced into large minimum-competence testing programs, funds may be reallocated at the lower level so that the funding for upper-level programs, such as APP, would be reduced.

☐ The new emphasis on minimum-competence testing and training might put such a crunch on the schools that they would need to increase the student-teacher ratios. This, of course, is very damaging to the AP Program, where the teacher-student ratio is smaller than in the regular classroom.

☐ If a college were not to allow CLEP credits, students in small high schools would be denied any credit-by-examination program because the school would be too small to have APP.

☐ There is a possible loss of revenue to the college if the student takes fewer courses because of credit by examination.

☐ Credit by examination can reduce the college costs for students if they can accelerate their programs. Will this mean that in a competitive recruitment time the colleges will bid against each other for the amount of credit offered to attract students or reduce credit to keep students on campus longer? The issue is holding power that keeps students either at the school level or at the college level for what might be called a normal tour of duty.

The economic concerns are summarized well in the earlier chapter by Douglas Windham:

> The greatest danger revealed by this paper's introduction to the economic issues in the debate is that financially the education community may face a "zero-sum" game. The benefits of credit exemption to the student may be purchased only at a cost to the education institution involved. In another zero-sum situation, higher education institutions may be tempted to expand early admission programs beyond justifiable limits simply to avoid the tuition losses resulting from other credit exemption programs. Finally, certain marginal institutions may become involved in the use of credit exemption as a competitive device against other, more responsible institutions. As in Gresham's law of monetary value — bad money drives out good — so, in an employment system increasingly dominated by credentialism, bad credits may drive out the good.

The following statements from the colloquium illustrate the many other problems encountered, some new and some continuing:

☐ Is there sufficient involvement of the faculty in the decisions regarding how much credit by examination will be counted toward degree programs?

☐ What are the key ways to have faculty not only involved but aware of what credit by examination is all about?

☐ The lack of clarity in the way colleges define what is allowed toward a degree from credit by examination is a continual problem.

☐ The fairly widespread lack of uniformity in the way colleges handle credit by examination results in inconsistent and vague college policy.

☐ The objective test format of so many of the credit-by-examination programs means that no written work is required, other than a student's name.

☐ The difficulty of educating the various professional schools about credit by examination and how it can or can not be used to evaluate admission beyond the baccalaureate degree is a consideration. Do professional school admission officers look differently on credit received by examination compared with credit received for courses actually taken?

Despite its many years, credit by examination still evokes anxieties and questions. The current environment may be different, however, and may even be less conducive to the expansion of credit options. Although some campuses have not yet considered credit by examination, others have been using it for many years. At the same moment it is a new and an old idea.

THE NEXT ERA

It does not seem possible to question that higher education in America is undergoing a metamorphosis. New and effective ways are being developed to educate beyond the formal classroom. The growth of credit by examination is not a fad built on whims; it is here to stay. A pluralism in postsecondary education goes beyond what we have known as higher education. Universities are becoming more flexible in their admissions requirements, course-distribution requirements, and demands for campus residence. We have seen state colleges change into regional state universities and have witnessed the dynamic growth of community colleges. Moreover, there is a growth of proprietary schools for vocational and technical education. Also expanding are the training programs sponsored by industry and labor unions, which currently might be the fastest growing postsecondary education. *The External Degree*, by Cyril O. Houle, is an excellent source of information about pluralism in education.[3]

Internal forces operating in colleges and universities will also cause changes. It is well known that the reduction of college en-

3. Cyril O. Houle, *The External Degree*. San Francisco: Jossey-Bass, 1973.

rollments during the 1980s is widely predicted. The competition for students will become exceedingly keen. The pressures for new programs and new procedures and the reactions to them are yet unknown. Figure 1, Live Births in the United States, illustrates in a simple way the enrollment problem that will be facing institutions. The graph is not based on any demographic theory, nor is it based on a set of assumptions. Rather, it shows the number of live births in the United States from 1957 to 1975 and the resulting decline in the potential college cohort of entering freshmen. The 1957 birth year is the source for the 1974–75 potential college freshmen. Note that the academic year 1977–78, following the 1960 birth year, is the beginning point for the decrease in live births. Thus, the 1980s is a period of decline in the typical college cohort. This is a fact—not a theory—that will have an impact on enrollment patterns of all types of postsecondary institutions. Add to this picture the growing pluralism in postsecondary education, and it is clear why there will be such competition for student enrollment among institutions during the entire decade. It is this climate that will affect the economics of credit by examination. It is difficult to believe that "school will keep as usual."

A dual pressure for change in our structured higher education procedures is upon us. Society is seeking greater access to higher education and varied programs, and institutions themselves feel internally the need to reallocate resources and seek adaptations to the changing enrollment picture. The 1980s will see new applications of the vast array of technological devices now coming on the market. These include videotape cassettes, videodisks, and small home computers that could easily be hooked into a central system through the telephone lines. The time will soon be here when we can electronically move information-knowledge from any point to any other point and thus directly into the home. It will be easy to move knowledge around rather than have it place-oriented, as we have considered it in the past. This will affect where learning takes place. The number of locations in which education can be acquired will surely increase in the 1980s. It will be possible to have teaching-learning wherever there is a telephone or an electric outlet.

In a recent issue of *The College Board Review*, there was a

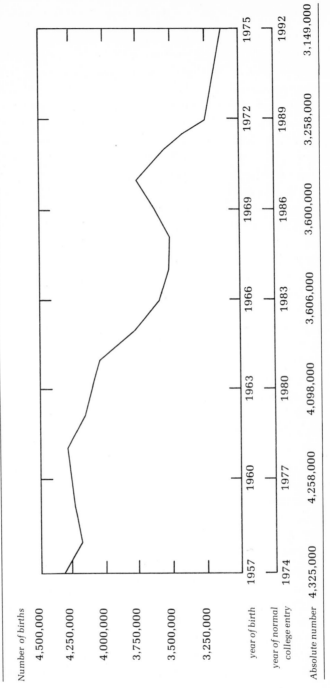

Figure 1
Live Births in the United States
1957–1975

Number of births

4,500,000

4,250,000

4,000,000

3,750,000

3,500,000

3,250,000

year of birth

| 1957 | 1960 | 1963 | 1966 | 1969 | 1972 | 1975 |

year of normal college entry

| 1974 | 1977 | 1980 | 1983 | 1986 | 1989 | 1992 |

Absolute number

| 4,325,000 | 4,258,000 | 4,098,000 | 3,606,000 | 3,600,000 | 3,258,000 | 3,149,000 |

SOURCE: *Statistical Abstract of the United States.*

presentation of the College Board's project Future Directions for a Learning Society. It was pointed out that there are approximately 58 million people now learning in our society today in one form or another and involved in educational activities. Of that 58 million there are only 12 million in the formal educational settings of kindergarten through the professional schools. This leaves 46 million in educational activities outside our formal educational system. It is this segment that will expand and request colleges and universities, as well as high schools, to furnish more flexible access to the credit and credential programs. It is already possible to acquire an academic degree from corporations rather than on campuses. How much this opportunity will increase in the 1980s is an interesting question to follow. The thought cannot be avoided that 46 million people involved in educational pursuits outside the formal system are going to be heard from. They will insist on receiving credentials and on getting on the academic record, or they more than likely will develop their own systems. This is already under way. The activities listed previously in this chapter show that some adaptation is already taking place in the Council on Assessment of Experiential Learning and the Office on Educational Credit of the American Council on Education. It should be noted also that the Department of Labor has been developing extensive educational programs through their Comprehensive Employment Training Act (CETA) and related youth activities. We seem to have a parallel system of public-supported education via the Department of Labor.

Nontraditional study is expanding in this country, and credit by examination is an integral part of it. The genie is out of the bottle, and we'll not get it back in the bottle, even if we wanted to. Credit by examination is a major movement in this country that cannot be denied; if it hadn't been invented, someone would surely do it now. It is in its earliest manifestations and will continue to expand. In Chapter 1 of this book, Donald Kreider says this extremely well: "Credit by examination will be reckoned as an educational innovation on a level with the establishment of land-grant institutions and the elective curriculum." The principal question that remains is: How well will we in colleges and high schools guide the further development of credit by examination to realize its best potential?

For many years higher education, structured on credits and credentials, has focused on time rather than on achievement. We now see developments in postsecondary education that portend significant changes for the future. The surge in numbers of adult students, many of whom are seeking not degrees but rather opportunities for self-advancement or development, will almost certainly cause institutions to offer or emphasize programs appropriate to those objectives.

The internal pressures from shrinking enrollments in the 1980s will add additional incentive for change. It is a time to re-examine the relationship of the knowledge and skills acquired in an educational program to the students' needs beyond their formal schooling. It is no longer productive to ask why we should have credit by examination; it is now necessary to ask in what directions it is proper for credit by examination to proceed.

Remembering the Dreamers

JACK ARBOLINO

Jack Arbolino directed two of the College Board's major programs—the Advanced Placement Program and the College-Level Examination Program—before becoming editor of the College Board Review. *Before joining the Board staff, he was associate dean of the School of General Studies at Columbia University and lecturer in English. He is the author of fiction for* The New Yorker *magazine and has written the book* College Learning Anytime, Anywhere, *with Ewald Nyquist and Gene Hawes, and educational articles for professional journals. He serves on the Advisory Board on Regents External Degrees of the University of the State of New York.*

When he introduced me, I was afraid Lorrin was going to present me as the only living Italian Aggie. But he didn't. Coming after the F group, I'm reminded of a story about Joe Mankiewicz, the Hollywood producer. When he was a student at Columbia many years ago, he started out as a premed. He had a very crusty professor of physics, and at the end of the year Mankiewicz got an F-minus. He went to his teacher and said, "Professor Farwell, I know I didn't do too well, but why did I get an F-minus?" Professor Farwell said, "Mr. Mankiewicz, I gave you an F-minus because I couldn't give you a G-plus."

Last week I participated in a phonethon—I suppose many of you are familiar with them. The college development office had us alumni down at the telephone company in a big room with a lot of desks with phones. You could call anybody: "Hi, we were just sitting around thinking of you and wondering if you could give us some money." It wasn't so bad, really. There were three of us from my class, and just in front of me was another volunteer, a young lawyer. He was calling his class, and would start every call with "Hi, there. This is a voice from the distant past." The developer came around and said, "Everything all right, Jack?" I said, "Will you please tell that guy to shut up or change his spiel?" The man turned around (and then he found out I was kidding). He was from the class of '74!

If his was a voice from the distant past, mine is a voice from the grave. I aged a lot in the last 24 hours, too. Listening to history does that. You remember the first night [of the colloquium], Fred Jackson alluded to the links between people and organizations. There are delicate, almost accidental shifts and changes that sometimes have a profound effect on a movement or a life. How did the Carnegie grant shift from the Commission on Institutional Cooperation to the College Board? I'll save my version of that for another time. But the point today is that history is made and changed by a thousand unconnected things that meet. The life that ended yesterday, but did not really end, began at all because a cutpurse from Dublin escaped unhung, or a girl from Calabria survived typhoid, or a young man left Copenhagen and ended up alive in Utah.

John Gardner and Frank Bowles were very important in the history of credit by examination, but the seeds of change were planted in many other places, by many other people, some here and some gone: people like Frank McKean in Utah, Paul Kelley in Texas, Doc Howe in Newton, Bill Cornog in New Trier, George Hall in San Diego, John Losak at Miami-Dade, Margaret Fagin, who took the tests to the candidates, and a wonderful colleague named Sam Kendrick, who knew the limitations as well as the value of tests. He used to say, "Hey, Jack, I hear there's a woman out in New Jersey who wants to take one of your tests." That's how we were scouring the land—we had four candidates at the first test administration, two in Atlanta and two in Chicago. A couple of years later, when we more than tripled the volume of the year before (21,000) and were up to 65,000, I said to him, "Hey, Sam, we just found two candidates in New Jersey." The seeds of change were planted by Caryl Kline and Connie Smith, by Harry

Weberman and Helen Clark, by George Dillavou at Roosevelt (how we worked the story of his student, the auto upholsterer who became a professor of philosophy), by Janine Webb, by Arthur Jensen, a distinguished, courtly man. He was the provost at Dartmouth and the head of the English department. To show you how dumb I was when I started in AP — dumber even than Harpo — the head of the English department asked me if I would go to Dartmouth because their English department wouldn't accept advanced placement. And I *went*. And I left thinking that if John Milton went to Dartmouth, he would have to take freshman English! I guess that's changed, but I wouldn't bet on it.

Changes were introduced by Hugh Lane, at the University of Chicago, and by Margaret Perry. Frank Bowles asked me to go to the University of Chicago — there's another example of my naïveté — to tell them about Advanced Placement; can you imagine? I met with the faculty committee and when I came back, Frank asked, "How did it go?" I answered, "I was politely eviscerated." He said, "You know there's nothing one Socialist hates so much as another Socialist."

Others who contributed were Richard Pearson and Florence Anderson, who had the vision to see beyond the sum of the numbers; Lorrin Kennamer and Dewey Stuit and Stan Idzerda and Ted Wilcox; Isaac Wirszup and Al Putnam and John Shirley. Important contributions were also made by Lee Medsker, Joe Cosand, Neil Turner, John Valley, and Louis Hacker, who went to England for a year and came back with a beautiful idea he couldn't sell; Joe Nyquist and Larry Chamberlain; Harpo, too, whose life did not begin when he came to the College Board (many of you don't know that he had a distinguished career before); Mother O'Byrne, Father Sullivan, and Brother Anthony. Twenty-one years ago at my first AP conference, I met Father Sullivan, a Jesuit, and Brother Anthony, a Christian Brother. We rode home together and as I got out of the car, Brother Anthony reached over and clutched my leg — he had gnarled fingers; he'd been a professional ballplayer — and as he grabbed me, he said, "Jack, don't let the Jesuits get hold of this thing or they'll swear they invented it."

The seeds were planted by Dyer, Keller, Dudley, and Serling; by Houle, Gleazer, Mendenhall, and Pagano; by Woodring,

Karling, Roundy, Brown, and Nolan — and by many others.

No one made CLEP, or AP, or credit by examination, but many helped and many now can say they find what happened somehow good.

Fifteen years ago a report to the trustees, recommending the establishment of CLEP, ended as follows:

"This program will focus on large divergent groups of students and will try to recognize and reward diversity of preparation as well as diversity of purpose. It will be based on a concept unpopular in many quarters; it will require considerable effort and expense; and it may fail.

"If the Council succeeds, the Board will be contributing to an important reconciliation in American education. Increasingly we seem to be seeking universal education and equality too. Maybe a clear intention, powerfully shared and executed with insight, initiative, and faith, can effect the equality of opportunity and the excellence we always promise. We are forever confronted with bristling alternatives: the liberal or the useful arts, the ivy or the junior college, past or present, God or man, a teacher like Barzun or credit by examination, the lists are endless and the rival claims are legion. But how do they bristle and how are they rival?

"We can begin by taking some things out of opposition; we can recognize the strength in diversity. It would be unrealistic to expect that one day the adherents of social responsibility and those of academic detachment will be truly reconciled. That may not even be important; but those who must worry about the whole of education, and the Board is among them, had better see the worth of both camps, for truly to treasure learning is to transmit it and see it used."

The trustees approved and CLEP was born. Well, I suppose in the end we might do well to remember what Joseph Wood Krutch said: "The proper observation we should make when we assay testing or any form of human endeavor is not Pavlov's 'How like a dog,' but Hamlet's 'How like a God.' " I don't know if this is history, but it's starting to sound like it.

Participants in the Colloquium

Jack Arbolino
Editor
The College Board Review
The College Board
New York, New York

Hugh M. Ayer
Associate Dean
College of Arts and Sciences
North Texas State University
Denton, Texas

Julia M. Bahrenburg
Academic Affairs Assistant
The College Board
New York, New York

Elizabeth Alvarez de Barbosa
Assistant to Assistant Secretary
    for the Academic Program
Department of Education
Hato Rey, Puerto Rico

Sherwood Barrow
Registrar
Simmons College
Boston, Massachusetts

Terry W. Bashor
Assistant Director of Admissions
University of Missouri — Columbia
Columbia, Missouri

Charles Bedford
Program Service Officer
College-Level Examination
    Program
The College Board
New York, New York

Theodore Bedrick
Registrar and Professor of Latin
Wabash College
Crawfordsville, Indiana

The Reverend George C. Bernard
Academic Vice President
University of Portland
Portland, Oregon

Daniel Beshara
Associate Director
Southern Regional Office
The College Board
Atlanta, Georgia

The Reverend John P. Betoni
Assistant to the Dean of the College
    of Liberal Arts and Sciences
Villanova University
Villanova, Pennsylvania

Charles W. Blaker
Headmaster, Upper School
Brookstone School
Columbus, Georgia

Harley Bradshaw
Psychometrist
Coordinating Testing Division
Southern Illinois University at
    Carbondale
Carbondale, Illinois

Raymond J. Brokamp
Assistant Superintendent
Cincinnati Public Schools
Cincinnati, Ohio

Charles P. Bruderle
Dean, University College
Villanova University
Villanova, Pennsylvania

Susan M. Byrd
Assistant Testing Coordinator
Old Dominion University
Norfolk, Virginia

Stephanie Calcagni
Academic Adviser
School of the Art Institute of
    Chicago
Chicago, Illinois

John A. Casey
Registrar and Associate Dean
Carthage College
Kenosha, Wisconsin

John T. Casteen III
Dean of Admissions
University of Virginia
Charlottesville, Virginia

Helen E. Clarke
Director
Special Advising Programs
University of Maryland
College Park, Maryland

Doris D. Claytan
Director of Instructional Services
School District of Greenville
    County
Greenville, South Carolina

Wayne Cogell
Assistant Dean
College of Arts and Sciences
University of Missouri — Rolla
Rolla, Missouri

Michael Contompasis
Headmaster
Boston Latin School
Boston, Massachusetts

Joseph J. Corry
Assistant Vice Chancellor and
    Director of Continuing Education
University of Wisconsin — Madison
Madison, Wisconsin

David H. Cox
Principal
New Trier High School, West
Northfield, Illinois

Robert L. Crawford
Associate Director of College
    Counseling
Phillips Academy
Andover, Massachusetts

Joseph L. Craycraft
Assistant Department Head
Economics Department
University of Cincinnati
Cincinnati, Ohio

Alan Crist
Associate Director of Admissions
University of Wisconsin — Madison
Madison, Wisconsin

Stephen E. Cvihar
Assistant Dean
New College
College of St. Thomas
St. Paul, Minnesota

Steve Dearnlan
Student
University of Wisconsin
Madison, Wisconsin

William J. Driscoll
Project Director
Committee on Institutional
  Cooperation of the Big Ten
  Universities and the University
  of Chicago (CIC)
Evanston, Illinois

Richard R. Dussault
Principal
Masconomet Regional High School
Topsfield, Massachusetts

Olga E. Englehardt
Chairperson and Professor
Department of Psychology
North Central College
Naperville, Illinois

Dalton D. Epting
Principal
Duval County School Board
Paxon Senior High School
Jacksonville, Florida

Celia Erickson
Associate Professor
Business and Administration
  Department
Saint Xavier College
Chicago, Illinois

Robley B. Evans
Academic Dean
St. John's Preparatory School
Collegeville, Minnesota

Glenn P. Fournet
Coordinator
Special Academic Programs
East Texas State University
Commerce, Texas

Richard W. France
Registrar
New Hampshire College
Manchester, New Hampshire

Judith Franks
Assistant to the Vice President for
  Academic Affairs
University of Tulsa
Tulsa, Oklahoma

Yvonne Freccero
Registrar
Smith College
Northampton, Massachusetts

Bruce J. S. Freed
Registrar
Bucknell University
Lewisburg, Pennsylvania

Geoffrey Freer
Chairman, Social Science
  Department
Coral Gables Senior High School
Coral Gables, Florida

Sue Froelich
Student
University of Wisconsin
Madison, Wisconsin

Lucien M. Geer
Director of Studies
Episcopal High School
Alexandria, Virginia

George Gilbert
Professor of Chemistry
Denison University
Granville, Ohio

Norman S. Gilbert
Director
Office of Testing Services
Northern Illinois University
De Kalb, Illinois

Jerry Girard
Associate Director of Records
Illinois State University
Normal, Illinois

Robert C. Goodman, Jr.
Headmaster
Trinity Episcopal High School
Richmond, Virginia

Ruth Gore
Director of Academic Advisement
North Carolina Agricultural and
    Technical State University
Greensboro, North Carolina

Margaret Gragg
Director
College Guidance Program
Charlotte Country Day School
Charlotte, North Carolina

Jessica C. Gunn
Assistant Director
Academic Services
Trinity University
San Antonio, Texas

Carl H. Haag
Program Director
Advanced Placement Program
Educational Testing Service
Princeton, New Jersey

Harpo Hanson
Program Service Officer
Advanced Placement Program
The College Board
New York, New York

David A. Harnett
Dean, Undergraduate Center
Nova University
Ft. Lauderdale, Florida

Allan C. Hartley
Educational Development
    Specialist
University of Wisconsin — Green
    Bay
Green Bay, Wisconsin

Dorothy Harvey
Superintendent of Guidance
Prince George Public Schools
Upper Marlboro, Maryland

Nancy L. Harwood
Assistant Principal for Instruction
Heritage High School
Littleton, Colorado

James Morris Hatch
Director of College Placement
The Harvard School
North Hollywood, California

Kaleem Hazer
Director
Testing and Test Development
San Antonio Independent School
    District
San Antonio, Texas

Peter Hoff
Student
University of Wisconsin
Madison, Wisconsin

Mary Lee Hoganson
Senior Counselor
University of Chicago
   Laboratory High School
Chicago, Illinois

Charles M. Holloway
Director, Special Projects
The College Board
New York, New York

James F. Hood
Provost
Lindenwood College
St. Charles, Missouri

Janet M. Hoover
Associate Dean
College of Arts and Sciences
Kent State University
Kent, Ohio

Sister Jean Cecile Hunt
Assistant Director of Academics
Siena Heights College
Adrian, Michigan

Sharon Ireland
Coordinator, Counseling
   Department
Minneapolis Public Schools
Minneapolis, Minnesota

Curtis M. Jackson
Director, Intra-Collegiate
   Academic Programs
Montclair State College
Upper Montclair, New Jersey

Fred Jackson
Director
Committee on Institutional
   Cooperation of the Big Ten
   Universities and the University
   of Chicago (CIC)
Evanston, Illinois

James H. Jaxon
Chairman, Mathematics
   Department
Terry Parker High School
Jacksonville, Florida

Warren F. Jones, Jr.
Dean, School of Arts and Sciences
Georgia Southern College
Statesboro, Georgia

Lois M. Kahan
Registrar
Brooklyn College
Brooklyn, New York

Maxine T. Kaiser
Director of Guidance
College High School
Bartlesville, Oklahoma

H. Paul Kelley
Director of Measurements and
   Evaluation Center
University of Texas at Austin
Austin, Texas

Lorrin Kennamer
Dean, College of Education
University of Texas at Austin
Austin, Texas

The Reverend Paul Kidner
Headmaster
St. Louis Priory School
St. Louis, Missouri

Ernest W. Kimmel
Director, Test Development
Educational Testing Service
Princeton, New Jersey

Caryl Kline
Secretary of Education
Pennsylvania State Department of
    Education
Pittsburgh, Pennsylvania

Donald Kreider
Professor of Mathematics
Dartmouth College
Hanover, New Hampshire

William J. Kritzmire
Associate Superintendent for
    Instruction
Southfield Public Schools
Southfield, Michigan

Henry C. Lacey
Acting Associate Dean of
    Academic Affairs
Dillard University
New Orleans, Louisiana

M. P. Lacy
Dean of Admissions and Records
Virginia Polytechnic Institute and
    State University
Blacksburg, Virginia

Nancy Lamb
Assistant Dean for Humanities
College of Arts and Sciences
Information and Advisory Center
University of Massachusetts
Amherst, Massachusetts

William T. Lenehan
Chairman, Department of English
University of Wisconsin — Madison
Madison, Wisconsin

John Losak
Dean of Institutional Research
Miami-Dade Community College
Miami, Florida

Fred W. Lott
Assistant Vice President
Academic Affairs
University of Northern Iowa
Cedar Falls, Iowa

Ann Lowery
Assistant Director of Admissions
North Carolina State University
Raleigh, North Carolina

Charles D. Lowery
Associate Dean of Arts and
    Sciences
Mississippi State University
Mississippi State, Mississippi

Eugene Lubot
Dean, College of Arts and Sciences
University of Tennessee at
    Chattanooga
Chattanooga, Tennessee

Caroline V. S. Luckie
Allendale Columbia School
Rochester, New York

J. Barton Luedeke
Associate Provost and Dean of
    School for Continuing Studies
Rider College
Lawrenceville, New Jersey

Robert E. McDonough
Associate Director
Midwestern Regional Office
The College Board
Evanston, Illinois

John J. McDow
Dean of Admissions and Records
University of Tennessee
Knoxville, Tennessee

The Reverend Richard McGarrity
Assistant to the Vice President for
    Academic Affairs
Marquette University
Milwaukee, Wisconsin

Brother John McGovern
Principal
Holy Cross High School
Flushing, New York

Franklin L. McKean
Dean, Student Affairs and Services
University of Utah
Salt Lake City, Utah

Barbara Maloy
Director of Admissions
St. Mary's Hall
San Antonio, Texas

John D. Margolis
Associate Dean for Studies
College of Arts and Sciences
Northwestern University
Rebecca Crown Center
Evanston, Illinois

Katherine W. Mille
Admissions Counselor
University of South Carolina
Columbia, South Carolina

Nancy Miller
School of Family Resources–
    Consumer Science
University of Wisconsin
Madison, Wisconsin

Patrick L. Miller
Registrar
Wheaton College
Wheaton, Illinois

John Noell Moore
Franklin County High School
Rocky Mount, Virginia

William C. Moran
Vice President for Academic
    Affairs
Frances Mary College
Florence, South Carolina

Barry Mussatto
Counselor
North Farmington High School
Farmington Hills, Michigan

Jack Myslik
Chairman, Mathematics
    Department
Colorado Academy
Englewood, Colorado

Leah Ellen Nance
Secondary Curriculum
    Coordinator
Clear Creek Independent School
    District
League City, Texas

Anne Nicholson
Registrar
Wheelock College
Boston, Massachusetts

George Nolfi, Jr.
President
University Consultants, Inc.
Cambridge, Massachusetts

Valters Nollendorf
Department of German
University of Wisconsin
Madison, Wisconsin

Gwen Norrell
Assistant Director
Counseling Center
Michigan State University
East Lansing, Michigan

Elbert W. Ockerman
Dean of Admissions and Registrar
University of Kentucky
Lexington, Kentucky

John J. O'Hearne
Director
Southwestern Regional Office
The College Board
Austin, Texas

G. Benjamin Oliver
Dean, Brown College of Arts and
   Sciences
Southwestern University
Georgetown, Texas

Diane L. Olsen
Managing Editor
The College Board
New York, New York

R. Thomas Ost
Registrar
Antioch College
Yellow Springs, Ohio

Edward Palmer
Associate Director
Middle States Regional Office
The College Board
Philadelphia, Pennsylvania

Thomas R. Papino II
Assistant Dean
College of Arts and Sciences
University of Miami
Coral Gables, Florida

Cecil L. Patterson
Vice Chancellor for Academic
   Affairs
North Carolina Central University
Durham, North Carolina

Mary H. Pease
College Counselor and Teacher
   of History
The Bush School
Seattle, Washington

Mitzi F. Perry-Miller
Director, College Parallel and
   Developmental Educational
   Program Planning and
   Coordination
Cuyahoga Community College
Cleveland, Ohio

Stephen L. Pfingsten
Department of Economics
College of St. Scholastica
Duluth, Minnesota

John T. Prentice
Executive Director
Student Administrative Services
University of Wisconsin—
   Whitewater
Whitewater, Wisconsin

Donna R. Pretty
Assistant Provost
University of South Carolina
Columbia, South Carolina

Joseph B. Price
Assistant Principal
Mount Lebanon High School
Pittsburgh, Pennsylvania

Alfred L. Putnam
Professor of Mathematics
University of Chicago
Chicago, Illinois

Sister Cathleen Real
Assistant Academic Dean
Barat College
Lake Forest, Illinois

Janelle Richards
Guidance Counselor
Glen Ridge High School
Glen Ridge, New Jersey

William F. Roark
Dean of Student Services
Georgia Southwestern College
Americus, Georgia

David P. Roselle
Secretary
The Mathematical Association
   of America
Virginia Polytechnic Institute and
   State University
Blacksburg, Virginia

W. Jess Rudiger
Chairman, College Counseling
   Department
New Trier High School East
Winnetka, Illinois

Lenore M. Saunders
Registrar
Montreat-Anderson College
Montreat, North Carolina

Joseph E. Schmiedicke
Director, Special Projects
Edgewood College
Madison, Wisconsin

Don Schroeder
Township High School District
Mount Prospect, Illinois

Victor Schultz
Student
University of Wisconsin
Madison, Wisconsin

Elizabeth B. Scruggs
Senior Guidance Counselor
Kingstree Senior High School
Kingstree, South Carolina

Rebecca Segal
Director
Motivation and Action Programs
The School District of Philadelphia
Board of Education
Philadelphia, Pennsylvania

John G. Severson, Jr.
Associate Dean, College of Arts
   and Sciences
St. Louis University
St. Louis, Missouri

Grace D. Shaw
Assistant Dean
L & S Student Academic Affairs
University of Wisconsin
Madison, Wisconsin

Walter Shea
Program Director
College-Level Examination
   Program
Educational Testing Service
Princeton, New Jersey

Betty B. Shemwell
Federal Projects Coordinator
Northwest Mississippi Junior
  College
Hernando, Mississippi

Leigh D. Sherrill
College Counselor
Georgetown Day School
Washington, D.C.

E. A. Sigler, Jr.
Principal
Highland Park High School
Dallas, Texas

Elizabeth J. Simpson
Dean
School of Family Resources–
  Consumer Science
University of Wisconsin
Madison, Wisconsin

Albert G. Sims
Vice President
Program and Field Services
The College Board
New York, New York

Leonard C. Siwik
Director of Guidance
Westlake High School
Westlake, Ohio

Jerome C. Sorensen
Director of Guidance
Wayne High School
Wayne, New Jersey

Ann J. Speer
Counselor
Marple Newtown Senior High
  School
Newtown Square, Pennsylvania

Richard N. Stabell
Assistant to the President
Admissions and Records
Rice University
Houston, Texas

Carl Stecher
Professor
Department of English
Salem State College
Salem, Massachusetts

Fred Stephens
Principal
Lincoln Senior High School
Sioux Falls, South Dakota

Robert E. Stoltz
Vice Chancellor
Academic Affairs
Western Carolina University
Cullowhee, North Carolina

Lee M. Swan
Assistant Dean of the College
St. Olaf College
Northfield, Minnesota

E. Nelson Swinerton
Director
Extended Degree Program
University of Wisconsin System
Madison, Wisconsin

Charles H. Tarpley
Director of Guidance
Hamilton High School
Memphis, Tennessee

William C. Taylor
Dean
Student Service
Brevard Community College
Cocoa, Florida

Victor C. Terek
Chairperson
Pupil Support Services
Conrad High School
West Hartford, Connecticut

Wilson Thiede
Provost
University Outreach
University of Wisconsin
Madison, Wisconsin

Thomas D. Tilson
Academic Dean
Northfield Mount Hermon School
East Northfield, Massachusetts

Charlene E. Tortorice
Testing Coordinator
Testing and Evaluation
University of Wisconsin
Madison, Wisconsin

John A. Valentine
Professional Associate for
    Academic Affairs
The College Board
New York, New York

Calvin A. VanderWerf
Professor of Chemistry
College of Arts and Sciences
University of Florida
Gainesville, Florida

Joan Vigdor
Assistant Registrar
Milwaukee School of Engineering
Milwaukee, Wisconsin

Michael Voichick
Professor
Department of Mathematics
University of Wisconsin
Madison, Wisconsin

Ann Vrtovec
Student
University of Wisconsin
Madison, Wisconsin

Sister Marie Wagner
Director
Counseling and Placement
Marian College of Fond du Lac
Fond du Lac, Wisconsin

Bonny Wallace
Director
College/Career Planning Center
Morton Watkins High School
St. Louis, Missouri

Jeannine N. Webb
Director
Office of Instructional Resources
University of Florida
Gainesville, Florida

Jerome C. Weber
Dean, University College
University of Oklahoma
Norman, Oklahoma

Henry Weberman
Counselor
Oak Park High School
Oak Park, Michigan

James H. Werntz
Director, Center for Educational
    Development
University of Minnesota
Minneapolis, Minnesota

John E. Westberry
Registrar and Director of
    Advisement
Texas Southern University
Houston, Texas

W. David Whiteside
District Coordinator
Township High School District 214
Mount Prospect, Illinois

Douglas Whitney
Associate Director
Office on Educational Credit and
    Credentials
American Council on Education
Washington, D.C.

Lee Wilcox
Associate, Academic Services
University of Wisconsin
Madison, Wisconsin

Frank Williams, Jr.
Assistant Director
New England Regional Office
The College Board
Waltham, Massachusetts

Wayne Williams
Director, Program Development
New York Regents Extension
    Degree
Cultural Educational Center
Albany, New York

Robert F. Willson, Jr.
Associate Dean
College of Arts and Sciences
University of Missouri
Kansas City, Missouri

Douglas M. Windham
Codirector, Educational Finance
    and Productivity Center
Department of Education
University of Chicago
Chicago, Illinois

Marie G. Wyatt
Assistant to Campus Principal
    for Instruction
Edina-East Secondary School
Edina, Minnesota

Al Zimmerman
Assistant Principal
Shaker Heights High School
Shaker Heights, Ohio